No More Pain!

Breaking the Silence of Self-Injury

Vicki F. Duffy

No More Pain!
by Vicki F. Duffy

Printed in the United States of America

ISBN 1-594675-42-2

Unless otherwise indicated, Bible quotations are taken from
the Nelson Study Bible, New King James Version (NKJV).
Copyright © 1979, 1980, 1982 by Thomas Nelson, Inc.

www.xulonpress.com

ACKNOWLEDGEMENTS

First and foremost I give all the thanks to God for where I am today. Nothing would be possible without His love, compassion, and healing power!

There are countless people that I would like to thank who have tried to help me over the years. Thank you to the many family members, friends, therapists, counselors, and doctors that tried to help me over the years. I extend genuine gratefulness and appreciation to all of those that prayed and never ceased believing in me.

I would like to especially thank my pastor, Ted Alleman for teaching me faith and leading by example what it takes to be a Christian. Also, thank you to all those at Living Praise Church for your prayers, love and support.

Thank you to JoAnn for reviewing this book and for new friendship. I would like to thank two very close friends; Charlene, for your countless hours spent proofing this book, reading, and re-reading, I appreciate your time and dedication; and Katrina for always listening to my never-ending stories and seemingly endless ideas, I appreciate your friendship.

To my mother, whom I love very much—all is forgiven—all is well.

And to my Chris, the husband of my prayers, you are amazing and I love you.

TABLE OF CONTENTS

A WORD FROM THE AUTHOR

You may be facing something that you feel no one has gone through, or perhaps that no person in this world could ever comprehend. I understand what it is like to have something devastating occur and to go through hardships; however, I now realize what it is like to have a great life. Throughout these pages, you will find support, information and answers on self-injury and a variety of other topics.

Self-injury was the most difficult thing for me to overcome. I will share what I went through, how I learned from it, and when I changed. And most importantly, at the end of each chapter you will be left with an encouraging story. My goal is to bring insight on what goes on with a person who puts his or her body through self-inflicted violence, as well as show you that anyone can overcome this!

The explanations given throughout this book, unless otherwise noted, are based on my personal experience. Ironically, I have never read any publication or article on self-injury. While writing this book, I referred to journal notations, letters written during hospitalizations, spoke with several people who knew me at the time I was harming myself, and retrieved medical records from hospitals and psychiatric units I was a patient of. What I am including in this book is only a portion of what I experienced.

It is my desire to share the goodness of God with everyone I meet. I am a firm believer that **good things can and will happen** no matter what a person faces in life!

The names of people mentioned have been changed for anonymity purposes. I have also changed the names to some buildings and locations and omitted medication names where I felt necessary. Chapters 1 and 2 introduce the concept and basics of self-injury, while the remaining chapters reveal my personal journey.

INTRODUCTION

I was born Victoria Marie Freund in Chester, Pennsylvania on September 10, 1968. In my short life, I had endured quite a bit of abuse. I had been molested and raped by a male acquaintance of my mother's at age 5; verbally and physically abused by my brother from ages 7 to 17, and sexually abused on and off from ages 11 to 13; and raped twice by an uncle at age 19.

I firmly believe that due to the abuse and sexual violence I endured, it led me into a path of destructive behavior and a life of utter confusion and feelings of inadequacy. I also believe that because I had a variety of unresolved issues, I later dealt with many problems and psychiatric disorders.

As early as 7 years old, I struggled with feelings of abandonment, low self-esteem, anger, fear, and hatred toward men. By the time I was 10 years old, I was hitting myself on a daily basis, was a bed-wetter, was attracted to girls, and had strong desires to be a boy. As I entered my teens, I often dressed as a boy, endured a sexual identity crisis and became self-destructive. In my late teens, I developed Anorexia and Bulimia, became an alcoholic, dabbled in drugs, was in and out of therapy, and entered the United States Marine Corp.

By the time I reached my early twenties, I was cutting specific parts of my body, was hospitalized for an eating disorder, diagnosed with a chemical imbalance, and dealt with suicidal tendencies.

By age 25, I was leading a homosexual lifestyle (which actively began at age 15), had brief involvement with a gang and became caught up in dozens of unhealthy relationships. I attempted suicide three times, had an abortion, and battled with mental illness. To add to this, I was daily taking 17 pills of psychotherapeutic medication, had skin graph surgery on both forearms (due to self-inflicted 3rd degree burns), accumulated over 250 scars from self-inflicted cutting/stabbing, and was in and out of psychiatric hospitals. As you can imagine, the medical bills were surmounting and I was forced to claim bankruptcy.

I was diagnosed with the following:

- *Borderline Personality Disorder (BPD)*
- *Dysthmia*
- *Major Depression*
- *Personality Disorder NOS and Mixed Personality Disorder*
- *Adjustment Disorder with depressed mood*
- *Anorexia Nervosa and Bulimia Nervosa*
- *Post Traumatic Stress Disorder (PTSD)*
- *Behavioral Disorder and Addictive Behavior*
- *Self-Mutilation/Self-Destructive Behavior*
- *Alcohol Abuse*

As I approached 27 years old, I was exasperated and felt as though I was just existing and taking up space. It seemed that whatever I tried was only good for a few hours, a day, and if I was lucky, sometimes a couple of days. I was at a point in my life where I desperately wanted to change, but didn't know how to go about the process of making it happen. Even though I thought I had tried everything possible to get better, nothing seemed to work and I felt defeated and helpless.

One Sunday in March of 1995, I was invited to a church service and I reluctantly went. It was my first time in over 15 years and it was unlike any church I had ever been to. From the moment I stepped through the doors, I sensed something different.

I sensed such love and peace; however, I thought it would be over once I left. I truly wanted so much to be normal, but had no clue how to do it. Everything else I had tried proved a failure and I was not ready to be let down again.

When I walked into Living Praise Church (LPC) in Florham Park, New Jersey, I felt great! I didn't remember ever feeling so much tranquility. I had never taken anything that ever made me feel so cool, calm, and collected. There wasn't any medication that had made me feel alert and alive; I knew it had to be something **real**.

Within days of going to LPC, I noticed that I had a little peace and the negative desires weren't as strong as they usually were. Even though I felt calmer, I wasn't quite ready to give God the credit. I was uncertain of my beliefs and not sure if I was ready for God, as I spent most of my life blaming and questioning Him as to why all this happened to me. I wasn't even sure if I believed in God. I knew there was something different, but couldn't figure out what it was. I remember looking up as if I was talking to God, asking Him if He was real. I didn't hear anything so I asked God that if He was real to give me peace. I noticed that I had peace and the anxiety wasn't as strong. The urges to harm were lighter and I was able to think a little bit clearer. Perhaps to an outsider that may seem so small of a change; however, for someone like me, it was a big thing just to see any change at all. It was at that moment that I knew for a fact that **God was real!**

A few weeks later I was given a Bible. I wasn't exactly sure what I was going to do with it, but I felt compelled to check it out. When I opened it, the pages turned to chapter 5 of a book entitled Mark. I began reading it and read about a man who had cut himself day and night and was miraculously healed by Jesus! I became very agitated and threw the Bible to the floor. I walked over to the Bible, stared at it for a minute, then picked it up and threw it against the wall in anger. *If God had really healed this guy, than why am I not in my right mind? If God heals, then why am I sick?* For over an hour I went back and forth 'talking' to God and throwing the Bible in frustration.

My 'talking' with God intensified to yelling. "*!@#* you God, if you are real, then why the hell can't you help me? Why can't you do for me what you did for that guy years ago? I'm tired, so tired of this !@#*, and tired of living this way. Don't you understand that I'm tired of crying all night long, cutting and drinking because I can't cope with anything? Life isn't supposed to be this way! I don't want mental illness. Please help me already!*"

I realize that swearing to God may not have been the best thing, but at that time I wasn't accustomed to talking with Him. After yelling at God, I pleaded with Him for help.

I had never been interested in God. If anyone ever mentioned God, I would wave my hand in the air, smirk and say, 'God, Shmod'. I never heard much about God. I didn't hear about anyone He helped nor did I see many people that He changed.

I figured that I had done everything possible to get better. It seemed as if nothing else worked, but I never thought of trying God because I mainly blamed Him. There was part of me that thought that what happened to me was His fault. Additionally, part of me wasn't convinced that He even existed. I wasn't sure what I believed in—not even certain about God.

Even though I had some questions, I figured God was my last resort. After all, God gave me peace for a few days. I thought I could at least give God a chance. I tried to put my doubts aside and immediately I began to talk to God. Actually, it was more of a debate or challenge. I told Him that I wanted answers and that I would give Him three weeks to 'prove' Himself to me. Even though I wasn't sure if I believed in God, I thought it would be a good idea if I at least put my efforts into it. I decided that rather than throwing the Bible at the wall, I might actually read it. I wanted my life to change but I still wasn't sure what I was looking for.

Until that moment I never dreamed it possible to have hope and a better way of life. Since the day that I "challenged" God, my life has never been the same!

What happened over the next 1 1/2 years was absolutely breathtaking! I started attending church on a regular basis, read the Bible, changed who I associated with, and started praying. With the love and mercy of God, I learned to cope with the past and look forward to the future. I realized that I didn't have to live my future based on my past. I have completely healed emotionally, recovered mentally, and overcome in every area of my life, as well as forgiven ALL the people who abused me!

God did not cause all that abuse to happen to me, and He is not the cause of bad things in anyone's life. Whatever was meant for bad in my life is now being turned around for good.

One of the many reasons I am sharing the details of my life is to bring awareness and insight of the possible after affects of any kind of sexual, physical and/or, mental abuse, habitual or one-time. For years I was in and out of therapy just trying to cope with the after affects.

I have stacks of medical reports stating various diagnosis that I was given, along with shocking doctor's statements. I spent many years in various types of therapy, on medication, and in and out of psychiatric units. I know without a shadow of a doubt that if it weren't for God, I wouldn't be where I am now!

Most of the problems I faced or the things I got involved in was a result of something that I needed to deal with. For example, although having an eating disorder and burning my body was harmful, that was not the problem. Those things were symptoms; they were outward manifestations of an inward problem.

There were countless times I would spend all day thinking about what was behind me. I would dwell on the past. I lived a life of the past. I could not think about the future because that scared me too much. At the same time I was terrified that the constant torment I was in would never end. So, because I feared the past, was terrified of the future, and dreaded the present, I felt like a prisoner, unable to escape 'my daily hell'.

I internalized my feelings and thought they would just go away with time. In actuality my feelings and thoughts only got worse, because instead of talking about them and dealing with them one at a time, I lived in constant torment, reliving the situations on a daily basis. Each time I would try to face an issue and admit I had a problem, all I could do was run from it. I had so much going on in my mind, that I didn't know what to deal with first. I was emotionally exhausted. Everything was overwhelming.

I used to ALWAYS ask myself:

"Why did this happen to me?"

"Why did God put me here?"

"Is the pain ever going to end?"

You may have asked yourself the same thing. I may not have all the answers to those questions; however, what I can tell you is that God does have a plan and purpose for everyone. And, yes, the pain will go away—permanently!

I hope that through reading this book, you will find that someone does understand and that you can get through a difficult time in your life. Everyone has the ability to overcome hardships and **you** can conquer what you may be going through right now. It is my hope that you will come to the realization that **nothing is hopeless!**

CHAPTER 1

SELF-INJURY 101

*It is my way of escape. It is my way to articulate thoughts
and emotions that I never could. It is my way to see and feel
the indescribable that is trapped inside. It is my method for
the throbbing ache to leave. When that cut or burn forms a
scar it is proof that there is pain. It is pain that others
cannot see or what they refuse to see.*

*That scar represents a battle wound, a wound from the
past. It is from a hurt that I cannot express in any other way
but through my own skin.*

This is what cutting and burning means to me.

Journal entry – summer of 1993

What It Meant To Me

Hitting. Slamming. Punching. Hair Pulling. This is what
I did. Cutting. Stabbing. Burning. This is who I became. It is
called Self-Injury, a term I never knew until a few years ago.
Although I intentionally inflicted hurtful things to my body
for 20 years, I never knew there was an official name for it. I
never read an article or book on self-injury, or heard anything about it. Since overcoming, I have been drawn to help
people who hurt their own body.

One day in March of 1999, I decided to look it up on a computer's search engine. I typed in 'hurting your body' and was directed to a self-injury message board. I began to talk with people of all walks of life who hurt their own body as a way of coping; young and old, men and women, married and single.

What is Self-Injury?

Self-injury is when a person causes intentional pain, harm and/or injuries to his or her own body as a way of coping or expressing overwhelming emotions. At times it can be brought on by an urge or impulse to cause harm as well as to receive instant relief, gratification, or satisfaction. Self-Injury is a **coping mechanism**, not a healthy one, but nonetheless it is a way for the person to express their emotions and get through the moment. I realize that causing self-inflicted violence is problematic; however, I believe it is a **distraction from coping with the current problem** and a distraction from dealing with the underlying issue.

Self-Injury is also referred to as: 'SI', self-harm, self-abuse, self-inflicted violence, and self-mutilation. Some people may even refer to themselves plainly as 'cutters'.

In my opinion a person who self-injures is greatly mis-understood. Most people who cause intentional pain and harm don't want to be figured out, they want to be under-stood. Although it is strange for a person to comprehend, self-injury is not only a coping mechanism, for some, it is a **way of survival**.

From my own personal experience as well as talking with others who harm themselves, the style or type of self-injury varies from person to person and comprises, but is not limited to the following: cutting, scratching, skin pick-ing, hitting, banging, chemical inhalation, and burning.

A brief description of the above mentioned styles or types of self-injury are as follows:

1) **Cutting:** By use of sharp knives, scissors, razor blades, glass, or anything sharp. Keep in mind that each injury can vary on depth and severity.
2) **Scratching:** By using fingernails, pins, needles, tacks, staples, plastic forks, pens, or knives.

Differences in Cutting And Scratching:
- A cut is a break in the skin that is usually made by something sharp and can have smooth or serrated edges. In some cases requires stitches.
- A scratch barely breaks the skin surface and is made by rubbing with anything pointed or rough. A scratch can leave a mark; however, it is considered 'superficial' and fades from a few hours to a day and does not leave a scar.

3) **Skin Picking:** Picking at old wounds, removing scabs, and/or interfering with the healing process of a wound.
4) **Hitting & Banging:** By slamming the body or a specific body part into a wall or any hard object, punching fists to head, legs, or face, hitting oneself with objects such as a hammer, brick, rock, etc.
5) **Chemical Inhalation:** Inhaling chemicals to the point of passing out or to experience a burning sensation or some sort of painful feeling.
6) **Burning:** By using chemicals, cigarettes, lighters, matches, candles, and/or branding.
   - A burn is tissue injury (skin) caused by exposure to extreme heat, extreme cold, electricity, acid, or certain other chemicals. Depending on the circumstances, the burn will vary: it may be relatively small and insignificant, or it may be very large and serious.
   - The severity is determined by evaluating the depth

and extent of the burn. Depth is based upon how hot the temperature and how long it had contact with the skin. Burn depth is classified as 1st, 2nd, or 3rd degree.

Symptoms of burn:
- 1st degree burns (mild) are usually red and painful.
- 2nd degree burns (somewhat deeper) are red, painful, and blistered.
- 3rd degree burns (deep) are usually pale/white, relatively painless, and may or may not be blistered.

Risks of 1st and 2nd Degree Burns:
Most 1st and 2nd degree burns heal within 2-3 weeks and do not produce any serious medical problems.

Risks of 3rd Degree Burns:
(a) Germs sometimes get into the wound and start to grow and multiply, producing an infection. (the chances of developing an infection vary greatly—depending on the severity of the burn)
(b) If the burn goes all the way through the skin, the area may require surgery in order to heal properly.
(c) Deep burns can leave a noticeable scar.
(d) Very large burns can lead to a host of serious problems that can be life threatening.

Awareness
The information I am including is to show the possible outcomes and severity of self-injury. Although you may not be able to get into the mind of someone who injures him or herself, this will give you a **better perspective** of self-injury and where the person is coming from. As someone who has overcome self-injury, I firmly believe that it is vital for people to have a complete understanding of what

self-injury is all about and what is behind it. (Those that injure themselves and those that are concerned for someone that does)

Some people have their 'favorite' area to harm on their body. Others have restricted areas, places that they won't cut. For example, I never cut my face or stomach. Some people may have their 'favorite' location to cut as well. For example, some people cut in the shower because it is easier to hide, as there is limited cleanup.

A person who self-injures may be described as:
a) A person who deliberately causes physical pain, harm, and/or injury to their body; even to the extent of causing breaks in skin, bruises, and/or marks that last for more than a few hours.
b) A person who causes any type of harm or pain to themselves as a way of coping with overwhelming emotions, negative thoughts, or past situations. (Whether they realize that is why they are doing it or not)
c) A person may or may not self-injure compulsively; however, find they are contemplating about harming their body even when things appear to be going well.

Self-Injury is not contagious. You cannot 'catch' it. Yes, there are things that can be influential; however, most likely a person is not going to start harming their body because somebody else does it.

Please note the severity of self-injury varies from person to person and regardless if it is 'minor' or 'major', it is not a healthy coping mechanism and is something that the person needs help with and much support to overcome. Just as the intensity and severity of self-injury vary, so do the reasons for causing such harm.

With the understanding that self-injury is a coping

mechanism, I believe that the following are **some reasons** why people may injures themselves.

Some Reasons A Person May Hurt Themselves:
- Avoid feeling
- Avoid showing emotions to another person
- Avoid appearing weak
- Embarrassment (real or imagined)
- Failure (real or imagined)
- Fear of abandonment
- For comfort
- Frustration
- Hate/hatred
- Inability to express themselves
- Instant gratification
- Overwhelming emotions such as anger, sadness, fear or guilt
- Punishment
- Reaction to a situation or upsetting news (real or imagined)
- Rejection
- Shame
- Taking on self-injury as a 'friend'—that it's the only thing that understands
- Way of escape
- When all other coping mechanisms no longer work

Most of the above mentioned were reasons that I subjected my body to some sort of self-inflicted violence. Many of the problems I went through were a result of something from my past that I needed to deal with. When I used to harm myself that was not the problem; it was an outward manifestation of an inward problem. The self-inflicted violence was the result of unresolved issues from an abusive life that needed to be dealt with.

Although it can pose problems in itself and is an unhealthy coping mechanism, self-injury is a form of **gaining control when things feel out of control**. It is also a way of coping with the past, the future, unbearable feelings, or everyday uncomfortable situations. For some it may also become a **way of survival**.

Again, the reasons why a person harms will vary from person to person. Some do it as a way of punishment, some to see blood, others for the pain; others do it when all other coping mechanisms just don't seem to work anymore.

Have you found out that someone you care about harms his or her body?

Although you may be experiencing feelings of hurt, disbelief, and/or are baffled by this, in most cases this is not a personal attack against you.

Self-injury, although highly misunderstood, is a way for a person to cope with outrageously overwhelming feelings at the moment. It may not be a 'healthy' or 'normal' coping mechanism, but it is one that the person knows and for whatever reason, they are comfortable with and can relate to. Please keep in mind that not everyone has learned how to deal with things normally nor have they learned 'normal' coping skills. Also keep in mind that cutting and burning can eventually become normal to the person doing it. It becomes part of their lifestyle and they may **feel lost without it**.

I have compiled some helpful tips that I believe will help you when talking with people who hurt themselves. These are tips of what **TO SAY** and **NOT TO SAY** to help the one you care about!

What <u>not</u> to say to someone who has recently told you they self-injure:

Just stop doing it!

Do you do that for attention?

We know you're in pain, but you don't have to prove it to anyone.
That is so disgusting, I can't believe you do that!
I can't believe you are doing this to me!
You're life wasn't that bad.
When you cut, you are hurting me more than yourself.
If you continue to do that, then you better get out of here!
I can't believe you do that to yourself, there are people in other countries that....

What to say to someone who has recently told you that they self-injure:

I may not understand why you do this, but I will try to help the best way I can.

When you are ready to talk about it, I will be ready to listen.

We will get through this together.

Do you think you can talk to me when you start to think about cutting?

Is there something that I can do to help?

I know this is hard for you—I want to try to help you.

You obviously don't like what they are doing, but LOVE the person, hug them, let them know that you are there for them. Do not isolate or punish them. Try to avoid giving ultimatums. If you are unable to handle what the person is telling you, then go to someone who is trustworthy who can talk to the person and who will be able to be supportive to him or her. As troubling as this may be to hear or odd as this may seem to you, it is often embarrassing and very difficult for the person to share this with you.

Are you someone who wants your son or daughter to stop?

Please remember that although you may be experiencing

feelings of anger and disbelief, this is difficult for your son/daughter to deal with as well. This is not a personal attack against you.

If you are a parent or guardian of someone who self-injures, you may be thinking of having 'no cutting guidelines' that your son/daughter must abide by. I don't think anyone likes to see the one they care about in pain and hurting themselves; however, putting strict guidelines and rules about not cutting will only put your son/daughter into a corner and into reclusion. They may become defensive and feel as if you don't understand. This may trigger them to then think that you don't care and they will automatically push you away. Please keep in mind that the self-injury is an **outward manifestation of an inward problem**. By putting demands on the person not to cut, you are focusing on the cutting rather than dealing with the problems that exist. This again will unfortunately only back the person into a corner. For some individuals, self-injury may become the only way they can deal with anything, to avoid feeling altogether, and a way to stay numb. **For some individuals, it may be too traumatic to experience feelings.**

Try and do other activities to get the focus off of him/herself. It is important for he or she to know they have your support. If your son/daughter feels that each time they make a mistake they get ultimatums and lectures, they may feel that they have no one to turn to and may stay in seclusion. Of course the goal is to no longer injure themselves, however, by telling them 'you can't cut' they may become distant and cut in secret.

Try to understand where they are coming from and try validating their feelings. You may not agree with how they see the situation, but that is how they perceive it. Be patient and love the person who is struggling and be as encouraging as you can.

How Are You?

The phone rings and you answer, and the person on the other end greets you saying, **"Hi, how are you?"** You might reply with, **"I'm fine thanks and you?"**

You walk into a grocery store and the cashier says, **"Hi, how are you today?"** You might look up and give a half smile and say, **"Fine."**

A friend asks you out for lunch and when you arrive to the restaurant, your friend says, **"Hey, how are you doing?"** You may look at your friend and say, **"Okay and you?"**

It seems that whenever someone asks, **"How are you doing?"** it is more of an automatic statement. No matter how a person is doing, it seems just as automatic for them to answer with "Fine", "Okay" or "Good". Is the person who is asking really interested in how the other is doing or is it more of a "let's do lunch" response? Think about it for a moment, when you ask someone how he or she is, are you ready for his or her reaction? Do you really want to know how they are doing? What if that person really is in need that day and you ask how they are and while you are asking you are thinking about your next sentence and overlook the situation?

Let's be sensitive to who we meet each day, and give a greeting with warmth. Whether it is someone you know very well or people you run into during everyday life such as the guy pushing your cart out to the car, the people drying off your vehicle at the car wash, the hostess at a restaurant, or the gas station attendant, let's show that we are interested in them. You might be surprised at the response you get, or better yet, how you will feel by making someone else smile.

It is amazing what a **little interest in another person can do for their self-confidence.** There is power of **life** and **death** in your words. A **destructive word** to someone who is down can be what it takes to destroy him or her. An **encouraging word** to someone who is down can lift him or her up, and be just what it takes to help them make it through the day.

We all have an opportunity to bring a little sunshine into the lives of every person we meet. Yes, this can happen with just a sincere, **"Hi, how is your day going?"**

Have a GREAT day!

CHAPTER 2

COPING – CONSUMPTION – ALTERNATIVES

Lately the feelings to hurt myself are intensifying. Thoughts are flooding my mind. I cut deeper than normal this week, and while they heal I'll switch cutting with smashing my head in the wall or punching myself. I don't want to give in to these thoughts, but I have to. I have nothing else that will take the pain away. Nothing else works. I desperately want help, but at the same time, I don't want to tell anyone what I'm going through. They will judge me, won't they? I think so. I know what I'll do—I'll only provide enough information to appease people. That will work. My situation is hopeless. No one really understands what I'm going through. No one wants to hear about this.
Who does?
Journal entry – October of 1993

Helping Your Family Cope

You may have other people in your household who are questioning why this person has scratches, cuts and/or burns on them. (Children, friends, etc.)

Let's say you have a son/daughter who has visible cuts or scratches on his/her body and your other children are asking you about it. The best thing is to speak to them on their level. (You would address a 5-year-old differently than a 13-year-old) Honestly explain the situation to them, again at the level you believe they can handle. Try explaining to them that their brother/sister is dealing with something that they feel they cannot handle and this is the way they are dealing with it. (Not a healthy way)

You could say something like this: "Your _____ (brother or sister) has _____ (scratches, cuts, bruises, burns) on his (or her) _____ (part of body) because _____ he (or she) is taking the problems out on _____him/herself. He/she is getting help and will be better soon."

It would sound something like this: "Your brother has scratches and bruises on his leg because he is taking his problems out on himself. He is getting help and will be better soon."

No person likes secrets and no matter the age of the child or person you are explaining this to, they will appreciate your honesty. The important thing to remember is that the children and adults who are around the person who is harming themselves need your love and support as much as the one who is cutting and dealing with the problems. It is important to be open and honest and to come close as a family and be supportive of one another. Keep that open line of communication, talk about the issues at hand rather than storming off; no yelling, no fits, no tantrums. Staying together and being supportive of one another will benefit everyone involved in the long run.

Whatever the person is going through now, they most likely did not get there overnight; the problems have been there all along, it just may have taken a particular incident for the problems to manifest. With that said, know that it will take a little time for the person to get a handle on things. Be patient and diligent to see things through.

The main thing is to keep the main thing the MAIN THING!

How Self-Injury May Begin

Many people who DO NOT harm themselves often wonder how another person could inflict pain on themselves. They may also wonder how they do it. It is very important for people to understand that there are negative thoughts, and other contributing factors that leads a person to act out. This is what I refer to as the 'pre-process'. If not in a controlled setting, I believe the more a person talks about the details of his/her cutting, it can possibly 'set the person up' for a scenario in their head and/or cause them to fantasize about further destruction.

I try to refrain from talking about the 'how to harm' and focus on the 'how not to harm'. There isn't much I can do about my scars, yes they are obvious, but I show them and talk about them as a way of bringing awareness to the possible outcomes of self-injury. I, in no way want to see anyone harm himself or herself further.

I believe certain destructive behaviors ultimately led me to a path of self-injury. I consider these behaviors as 'warning signals' and to show possibilities in progression of behaviors. I believe that if not caught early on, self-destructive behavior can lead to more serious things such as self-injury.

As young as 8 years old I began hitting myself. I would punch a wall, bang my head against a wall or hard object, punch my face, and hit any hard object to the point of feeling numb. (I hit myself on and off for over 15 years).

When I was 12 years old, I started to have many negative thoughts about hurting myself. I had thoughts of running in front of a car or truck and lighting myself on fire. I didn't understand why I was thinking these thoughts. I didn't want to die. I thought I deserved to feel some sort of pain or punishment and wanted to reprimand myself in some way.

Between the ages of 13 and 14 years old, I was suspended from school quite a few times and got into fights.

When I was 14 years old, I pulled out hair from on top of my head which created a very visible bald spot, about 4" long and 1 1/2" wide. I did this for about a year where my mother took me to a doctor as she was convinced that I had some sort of hair disorder. I wasn't sure why I did this, what was wrong with me, or what I was going through. I felt that I couldn't tell anyone and knew nobody would understand.

When I was 15 years old, I began to cut chunks of hair from my head. I tore out small chunks and would wear a hat to hide the bald spots.

When I was 16 years old, I began to shave hair from my body. I shaved off all the hair from my entire body with the exception of my head.

One afternoon after school when I was 18 years old, I started hearing strange sounds and voices and took off my braces with a pair of pliers.

By the time I was 19 years old, I was battling with an eating disorder, mental disorders, and acted out in various unhealthy coping mechanisms, through age 27.

In my early 20's I began to have thoughts of causing permanent physical damage to my body. I remember thinking that I wanted some sort of mark on the outside of me that would match the pain I felt inside. One night I decided I would cut myself with a butcher knife, which later led to cutting with razors and other sharp knives. Within a few months it led to burning.

I consider all these destructive effects as symptoms of a deeper problem. As mentioned previously, I believe like me, if not caught early on, it can lead to much more serious behaviors.

There were 2 'reasons' that I began to cut and burn myself:

1) All the other things, although inflicted some sort of pain, they were temporary fixes that didn't last.
2) I wanted something visible and permanent to match the pain and emotional scars I had inside.

Mixed Emotions & Consumption

I know many of the mixed emotions that go along with and follow self-injury. The emotions before, during, and after can be tremendous in itself. I know some people can get to a point where they don't even want to feel—they just want to be numb. I have a very good idea of what a person who injures him/herself might be thinking; that they will never get through this—but I know you will overcome this once and for all. It may seem horrific and never-ending right now, but it won't forever. **Your situation will turn around**.

I understand what it feels like to be **consumed** by cutting and burning. I understand what it is like to never see an end. I know what it is like to really believe that harming yourself is the only way to resolve anything. I know what it is like when it becomes the reason you are alive—it goes from coping to being. I know. I understand. I relate. I know what it feels like to get in a place that I called 'the zone', which is no matter what anyone said or did, my mind was made up that I was going to do serious damage. 'The Zone' was a place in my mind that I would go alone and where nobody existed. I would get to a place in my mind where I would think only of harming. I would fantasize on what I would carry out. I would have imaginations in my mind. It was a place that no matter what anyone said or what the circumstances were, I was going to hurt myself and there was no deviating from that. There was no considering alternatives or other options.

There was nothing that would stop me.

In my experience it seems that people didn't know what to do with me. It seemed that people understood eating disorders or alcoholism, but when it came to me cutting and burning, most were thrown for a loop. I felt that therapists and psychiatric doctors had a better understanding of those things and therefore couldn't help me. There were only two people who attempted to understand me when I was in the midst of cutting and burning. It was my mother and my therapist, Jan. During therapy sessions, Jan would ask me why I cut on that particular day. By the time she asked me I no longer remembered, so I didn't share any information. I didn't share my plans or ideas, I kept it all to myself. It was my secret.

As a result of 'blackouts', there are many details of my cutting and burning that I have no recollection of. I had blackouts when drinking alcohol and without. I retrieved certain incidents from my medical files, police reports, and talking with those who knew me. I know that there are many people out there who are going through and doing what I went through, if not worse. Although at the moment, I was convinced that causing physical injury made me feel better, it actually made things worse: going into a vicious cycle of harming, guilt, and mental torment. I now know that cutting, burning, and all the negative things I did, as a way of coping didn't work.

Beyond Coping

In my opinion for a person to habitually self-injure, it can go beyond a coping mechanism. I believe they are someone who is either:

a) Experiencing various overwhelming issues and harms as a way to escape the moment

b) Using it as a way to be numb to avoid feeling—if numb they cannot feel the pain of the issues at the moment

c) Reacting to anything—it becomes 'being' instead of coping

d) All the above mentioned

Ten years ago, I thought I would always be struggling and accepted that harming myself was part of who I was. **That was a lie in my mind I chose to believe.** Anything destructive should not be a part of any person's life.

If you are someone who is totally overwhelmed and cannot even think of anything but harming, all I have to say is to **try to take things slowly.** Do the best you can to try to not let things consume you. Think of it as baby steps; take things one minute at a time if needed. Try not to act out on those overwhelming emotions that you sense at the moment (anger, hate, sadness, frustration, etc.). Try. Some people think that trying is nothing, but it is something. At least by trying, it shows you are making an attempt, and for many people that is a step in itself. Please don't give up on yourself; you can get through this!

If you are someone who causes physical harm to your body:

Try and take a step away for a moment and think things through. Realize that you do not deserve any more pain. You do not need physical scars to match your internal scars and the pain you feel. Understand that stepping away for a moment is a 'temporary fix'. In order to prevent future incidents, you have got to get some alternatives. Think of alternatives in advance, prior to thinking of acting out. By having an alternative and staying busy, that will keep you active and help to prevent your mind from wandering off into thoughts of destruction. If you have some alternatives ready, than that will help you the next time you 'feel the need' to cut, burn or beat up on yourself. I am an absolute believer that anyone can stop harming his or her body! It may not be easy at times, but it can be done!

Alternatives to Hurting Yourself

From my own personal experience as well as talking with people and visiting them in psychiatric units, it seems that the doctor's answer to the problem was to prescribe medication. Medication may help with some urges and impulses, but in my opinion it is in **no way a permanent solution**. If the issues and problems are not dealt with, than people may harm themselves while on medication. For example, I continued to harm myself while on medication and under psychiatric care. When something triggered me or bothered me, I would revert into what I felt safe with and nothing could hold me back.

Some of my cuts and burns were pre-meditated. I got preoccupied with the meticulous details. Other times I cut as a reaction and something that was an instant way of escape. When relating to alternatives one has to **make a conscience decision that he or she is going to allow that alternative to work**. I believe that the alternatives I am sharing will work if thought out and planned. Think about it for a moment: cutting, burning, and hitting 'works' because it brings instant gratification, it is easy, it is something that you can just react with, and it doesn't need to be thought through.

I have heard about a variety of alternatives from holding on to ice, to snapping a rubber band against your wrist. I am not sure if they work or not because I only heard of them after I stopped. It will help if you have an alternative before you explode and prior to acting out on yourself. Many of the coping mechanisms I am mentioning, I have thought of over the last few years. If I had thought of them while I was in the midst of harming, perhaps they would have helped me. There are some coping mechanisms that work right away and others that work over a period of time. You will need to work on **conditioning yourself to be open** to new ideas and

changing your way of thinking. Try and let go of the idea that self-harming is the only thing that brings relief.

Here are a few alternatives to try:

1) Create A Burden Box!

Wouldn't it be great to get rid of a problem right away? It's quite possible that we could all answer YES to that question! Here is a suggestion that a friend of mine told me really works.

- Take a brown shipping box or a shoebox and cover it with colored paper or newspaper.
- Tape the box all over with clear tape and cut a slit on top. The slit should be just big enough for a slip of paper not to come out.
- You can write on the box, put photos on it, draw pictures over it, or decorate it any way you like.

The purpose is for you to write down on paper your problem, issue, situation, or whatever you are upset about or dealing with at the moment. The paper represents the problem. After writing it down, place it in the slit on top of the box. The slip of paper with the problem is to remain in the box. By placing it in the box, you have begun to give your burden away and by it being out of sight, it will start to leave your thoughts. Give your problems to God, as He does care for you!

2) Music Alternatives!

You know the saying, "You are what you eat?" Well, you are also what you listen to. Did you ever really pay attention to the lyrics of the music you hear? You may think the person singing is awesome because they can identify with your pain, but if all they do is sing about misery, how good can that really be? The music you are listening to may not be the most positive and you might need a change. Try switching what you listen to.

3) For Anger!
- Get a punching bag and kick and punch away
- Get a boxing bag and hit and punch to get out your aggression

4) Do Other Things When All Your Thoughts Are About Harming!

Sometimes the thoughts flood your mind and you spend a lot of time thinking about it even though you are not actually cutting. If you spend time doing other things, it will keep you from thinking and obsessing on hurting yourself.
- Call a friend who will lift you up
- Draw or paint a picture
- Go to the gym and work out
- Go out with good friends that are positive influences
- Go shopping
- Get a pet—it will be something to take care of and take your mind off yourself
- Help a friend with a project (building, volunteer, etc.)
- Listen to encouraging music
- Learn to ask for help
- Take your kids out to a park
- Write in your journal or write a letter

5) Take Time To Express Your Emotions!

If you keep on harming every time you have an overwhelming emotion, you will continue to avoid feeling because you are using it as a way of escape.
- Let yourself cry, scream, or vent in a healthy way
- Allow yourself to feel emotions that you normally hide
- Talk with someone when you feel the desire to hurt yourself

6) Be Honest With Your Therapist!

Try and help the person who is trying to help you. Remember that you are going to counseling for yourself, not the therapist.

- It would be a great idea to go there ready and willing to be honest
- Avoid telling your therapist what you think they want to hear

If you are not willing to meet them half way or are not honest with what is going on, then counseling may not work.

7) Throw Out Your Favorite Things!

It is important to get rid of the tools you use to cause destruction on yourself.

- Throw out the things you use to cut or burn
- Throw out your favorite knife or favorite cutting objects
- Get rid of the stuff that you have hidden in 'safe places'

Of course you can buy more, but if you don't have it on hand, it will help prevent you from doing it at the moment. You will help yourself to avoid doing it as an instant answer. Harming yourself cannot continue to be your safety net. Until you give it up, you may continue to have problems because instead of dealing with the problem, you are escaping the moment. It's difficult, but let go of what you know!

8) Cover Yourself!

If you have a certain area on your body designated for harming, think about covering that part or area. If it is covered, you won't be looking at it all the time. This will help you to avoid obsessing over it.

9) Help Your Skin Heal!

Take care of your wounds by keep them clean. Keep cuts and burns bandaged to help the healing process and to avoid picking at them.

Begin to take care of your skin by applying healing aids such as antibiotic creams, vitamin E oil, or cocoa butter.

If you are trying to help someone:

It will require much love, support and patience on your part. Most people don't really 'want' to harm themselves, it is something they have gotten accustomed to doing, and/or have convinced their minds that it's the only thing that will take away their pain. Most people have a hard time 'talking it through' with others. Assure the person that you are there for them when they are able to talk about it. In the meantime, you may want to find a supportive person to discuss this with. The best thing is to pray to God for the person you care about.

Be Encouraged!

I would be doing you a disservice if I didn't tell you that there is someone who heals. The following is an excerpt from the Bible. It is about an individual who was healed and set free of cutting his body and mental illness!

And when He (Jesus) had come out of the boat, immediately there met Him out of the tombs a man with an unclean spirit, who had his dwelling among the tombs; and no one could bind him, not even with chains, because he had often been bound with shackles and chains. And the chains had been pulled apart by him, and the shackles broken in pieces; neither could anyone tame him. And always, night and day, he was in the mountains and in the tombs, crying out and cutting himself with stones. When he saw Jesus from afar, he ran and worshiped Him. For He said to him, "Come out of the man, unclean spirit!" Then they came to Jesus, and saw

*the one who had been demon-possessed and had the legion,
sitting and clothed and in his right mind. And they were
afraid. And when He got into the boat, he who had been
demon-possessed begged Him that he might be with Him.
However, Jesus did not permit him, but said to him, "Go
home to your friends, and tell them what great things the
Lord has done for you, and how He has had compassion on
you." And he departed and began to proclaim in Decapolis
all that Jesus had done for him; and all marveled!*
The Bible, Book of Mark,
Chapter 5, verses 2-8, 15, 18-20

This man was healed from a life of torment! Although
this man was demon possessed, that does not mean that just
because you cut you are full of demons. When I first read
about that man, I totally identified with it. Causing any type
of self-inflicted violence is not good and you can be healed
from doing this. Even though I wasn't sure if I believed in
God, I was amazed that someone could be healed of something that I was in the midst of. You may say, "I don't believe
in God!" but that does not stop God from believing in you!

Jesus told that man to go tell his friends what great
things the Lord had done. When I was healed, that became
my desire. This is exactly my aspiration; to go and tell
people what Jesus has done for me. Wherever I go I tell
people that He heals anyone of anything, anytime. There
may be times that a person needs to be ready and willing,
but **God can and does heal!**

CHAPTER 3

INNOCENCE BROKEN

My mother did everything she could for me…I know she
tried. I don't know why she allowed him over; I have no
clue. But she did. It isn't her fault. She didn't tell him to do
that, but she could have prevented him from being there.
Right? I don't know. I love her though. She makes me crazy
sometimes. How could this happen? I don't know,
but it did. If she could change what happened
she would. But it can't change.
It's over, but is it? I think about this so much
that my head hurts.
Journal entry – July 17, 1987

The Early Years

My parents had gotten divorced when I was 4 years
old. I always appeared to be a very happy go lucky
kid. It appeared that I would bounce back from most
anything. I enjoyed being around people and liked to be the
center of attention. I was very appreciative of the little
things in life and loved my mother beyond comprehension.

In 1974, when I was 5 years old, my mother had obtained custody of my brother and I and moved us to Seaside Heights, New Jersey. We stayed temporarily at a hotel called the Cetza, the first place I had been to in New Jersey.

Too Young To Be Alone

Within a few weeks, we moved down the street to a place of our own and my mother enrolled my brother and I into elementary school. I was in kindergarten and met Shannon who soon became my best friend.

My mother was beautiful and it seemed that she attracted every man wherever she went. She had many male friends, whether she dated them or not, men would be over the house fairly often. One friend, Ron who liked my mother was always nice to us and my mother thought it was great for my brother and I to have a father figure. He would bring me presents, play with me, and have me sit on his lap.

One evening after my mother and Ron had gone out drinking, he came to the house and stayed overnight. Ron came into my bedroom and woke me up. I recall him smelling, but am not sure of what. He asked me if I liked lollipops and became excited because I liked candy. He asked me what my favorite flavor was, I told him cherry. He told me he had a lollipop for me. He proceeded to take off his pants and told me to suck the lollipop. I told him that I didn't see a lollipop, and he shoved his penis in my mouth.

I started to cry and he told me everything would be okay.

He told me to sit by him on the bed. He put his hand inside my underwear and then put his fingers inside me. I was frightened and told him to please stop. I had to go to the bathroom, and he told me the only way I could go was if I replaced his fingers with my own.

As I walked to the bathroom, he told me that he was watching me and to come right back. The bathroom door was in clear view of my bedroom door so he could see me.

As I urinated, it hurt so badly that I started to cry. I heard him whispering telling me to be quiet.

"Sshhh," he whispered.

I wanted to run out to my mother but I was terrified. I went back to my bedroom and he put me on the bed. He removed my underwear and undershirt and got on top of me.

When he was done, he got up, snarled at me and said, "Don't tell your mother, don't you tell anyone."

I just stared at him and cried. He put his hand over my mouth.

"You be quiet and don't tell anyone, especially your mother. If you tell anyone I will kill your mother. I will kill your brother. I will even kill your dog."

I looked at him and just shook my head up and down.

So, I didn't tell.

About six months later my mother realized she had a drinking problem and began going to a recovery program. She was doing well and had stopped dating Ron. Since I had not seen him around, I gained the courage to tell my mother what he had done to me. I was 6 years old, but I finally did tell her. She told me that she was very proud of me for talking to her and that I did the right thing. She was furious with what Ron did.

A few months prior, I had been missing for half a day (unrelated incident) and the police were involved. One of the police officers on the case, mentioned to my mother to contact him if she ever needed help with anything. My mother remembered what that police officer said and contacted him for his advice on the situation. He explained to my mother that putting a child through a trial like that would be very difficult. She decided not to file a complaint or press charges against Ron.

My mother went to Ron's place of work to see him, but he was not there. She bumped into his business partner and told him what Ron had done. He couldn't believe what she was telling him. We never heard from Ron or saw him again.

My mother took me to a counseling facility where I was assigned to a therapist, Miss Halton. I saw her for months but never verbalized the incident to her. I illustrated what Ron did to me through pictures. Miss Halton had given me two dolls and asked me to show her what happened and I did.

As Years Passed

As years went on, I had terrible nightmares of Ron. I also had continuous thoughts and hopes that he would die. I often wondered what happened to him and if he had ever gotten punished for what he did to me. I never understood why he wasn't punished and got the message that what he did was okay.

As I got a little older, I asked my mother to tell me what happened to Ron after I told her what he did to me. My mother explained to me that when I told her what occurred she was infuriated with what he had done but was not sure what to do, as she didn't want anything to happen to us.

Many years later, my mother told me that she found out that Ron had died of cancer.

At that young age I may not have understood why that happened, but I knew that it was wrong. I know that even though I couldn't change what occurred; as I grew older I could have chosen to move on with my life. As the years progressed, I spent an enormous amount of time and energy hating Ron for what he did. I believed my hatred toward him was justified. I soon came to the realization that I couldn't go on hating and that I could have spent that negative energy in a more positive way.

Forgiveness Is The Key!

I had unforgiveness toward my mother for years. I thought she should have done more to protect me. I had much resentment toward her, but I forgave her.

Over the years, a lot of hatred built up from what Ron did to me. It wasn't until **21 years later** that I forgave him for what he did. That is a long time to hold onto something like that. It's never too late too forgive someone.

I realized that I needed to forgive him so I could go forward with my life. If anyone has hurt you in any way, you may believe that forgiving those who hurt you is the most difficult thing you could do. I believe **forgiveness is key to healing**. Although you may think that forgiving someone is unfeasible right now, soon you will see that ALL things ARE possible.

Forgiveness can be difficult, especially if you have been abused, hurt, betrayed and/or lied to. However, no matter how you may feel, forgiveness is the key to opening that door that has been locked for a long time. You may have gone through some horrible and traumatic things and you cannot ever see yourself forgiving that person or what he or she has done. You may feel that it is way too hard to forgive, and that may seem true at the moment; BUT you can forgive. **Forgiveness is an act of your will. It is a choice to forgive someone.** Remember, you choose to forgive and let go of the unforgiveness you have clenched your hands on toward another person.

You may even feel that the person doesn't even deserve to be forgiven, and they may not, but forgiveness is for you, not the other person. It will bring healing and restoration. We all need to forgive. You need to forgive the person or people that have harmed you or abused you. If and when you continue to hold unforgiveness in your heart, it may be the very thing that ties the hands of God and keeps healing from being manifested in your body.

When you release that unforgiveness and forgive that person or those individuals who have hurt or abused you, and turn all of the past over to God, your healing will come!

Forgiveness is not saying what the person did was right

and it is not condoning what the person did, forgiveness is mercy. **It is giving mercy to the guilty**.

Unforgiveness ultimately only hurts you, not the other person. It can and does fester inside like a deadly disease. It is you that makes the conscious decision to release the anger, hate and bitterness from your heart that you have toward that person who harmed you. When you forgive, God will remove the feelings of unforgiveness, and replace it with love and compassion in your heart toward that person. There is hope for all relationships, they can be restored and hurts healed.

You have the ability to forgive. Sometimes we think that we could never forgive the people who hurt us (whether rape, mental or physical abuse, etc.). What is amazing is that Jesus forgave all those who mocked, rejected, and eventually killed Him. *"Then Jesus said, "Father, forgive them, for they do not know what they do." The Bible, Book of Luke, Chapter 23, verse 34*

If you find yourself getting bitter or judgmental about what someone has done or said to you, just know that **forgiving the person is your step to freedom**. Ask God to help you forgive, and He will. That is the first step in going forward. This can be difficult and can be heart wrenching and tough for your mind to understand, but there is freedom in forgiveness.

"Therefore I say to you, whatever things you ask when you pray, believe that you receive them, and you will have them. And whenever you stand praying, if you have anything against anyone, forgive him, that your father in Heaven may also forgive you your trespasses. But if you do not forgive, neither will your father in Heaven forgive your trespasses."
The Bible, Book of Mark, Chapter 11, verses 24-25
Remember this—forgiveness is mercy—not justice!

CHAPTER 4

WHEN IT'S A SIBLING

Dear mommy, 11:15 pm I washed the dishes because my brother said that I was lazy and didn't vacuum correctly and that I made all of the dishes dirty. So he said that he would only do half. Don't worry, I am not complaining about it. I cleaned my closet, room, living room, and did the dishes. Please wake me up to go to the bathroom tonight. Thanks. Sorry I was such a grump today. Love ya! P.S. Wake me up as early as you get up. P.S.S. DON'T BE DEPRESSED! Love, Vicki Letter to my mother – June of 1978

A Never-Ending Challenge

Growing up with my brother seemed like a never-ending challenge. It was an ongoing endeavor of keeping up with his mischievous behavior. He was a bully and always wanted his way, and never settled for being told no. If I didn't play or do things exactly as he wanted, or if it didn't go just as he had planned, he would get angry. In order to get his way, he would push me around, make fun of me, trip me, and pull pranks. He would call me names like jerk, stupid, ugly, and idiot. He seemed to get so much amusement seeing me get upset.

Whenever adults were around, he would act differently. It would look as if I was instigating a situation when, in actuality, he had just done something to me and I was reacting to him.

My brother was adored by family members, which made it much harder on me. My brother was good looking and I felt like the ugly duckling. I felt rejected.

Going For A Ride

During the summer of 1976, when I was almost 8 years old, my mother, brother, and I spent the day at her boyfriend's house in Seaside Park. I went outside to walk along the beach by the bay. My brother met me outside on his bicycle. He wanted to have a race and I told him that I didn't have my bicycle with me. He said he wanted to race on his bike while I ran. I told him that I didn't want to run and wanted to walk by the sand. He was riding back and forth in circles asking me to race.

"I want to race!" he demanded.

"I don't feel like racing," I said.

"I want to race!" he yelled.

"I don't want to!" I shouted.

"If you don't race me, I'm going to run you over!" he yelled.

"I don't want to race!" I yelled to him. I continued to walk. I was getting close to the house, so I started walking on the side of the street.

My brother sped away.

"You better start running!"

"Leave me alone!" I turned and yelled back. As I continued walking, I suddenly heard a whooshing sound and turned around and saw my brother right behind me. *Oh my gosh, he really is going to run me over!*

I started to run and heard thrashing sounds from behind me. As I began to look behind me, I suddenly got hit and plummeted to the ground. I landed face first into the street; my teeth were full of tar. I was bewildered, extremely upset and began crying.

My brother ran me over with his bicycle. He said he would do it and he did.

My mother came running out and I heard my brother yelling to her.

"I told her to run. I thought she'd get out of the way," he said convincingly.

There wasn't anything I could mutter, as my mouth was bleeding and I was crying. I was rushed to the hospital and had broken my two front teeth.

Ready For Anything

It seemed that no matter how nice I was or how much I did for my brother, he would always end up being unkind to me. At times, it appeared as if he actually enjoyed himself.

When I was 8 years old, I felt angry and began hitting myself. I would punch my fists into a wall, bang my head against a wall or hard object, punch my face, and hit any hard object to the point of feeling numb. I hit myself on and off for over 16 years.

I was afraid of the dark and always kept the lights on in the room I was in. My brother would turn off the lights and laugh seeing me run to turn the switch on. There were times that when I would be in the shower, he would come in and turn the lights off. By the time I screamed, he had already ran out of the bathroom. I would jump out of the shower to turn on the light. Other times he would hold the door to the room I was in so I couldn't get out.

Being a Human Punching Bag

When I was around 9 years old, my brother became

more domineering. Whatever he wanted he would get. He eventually started threatening me. "If you tell, I will..." became his motto. It always ended with 'beat your face in' or 'punch you in the stomach'. I didn't think it was right that he treat me like this, so one night I told my mother how mean he was to me and that if he didn't get his way, he would hit me. She had a talk with him, and since then, every time she wasn't around he would kick me, punch me or shove me into a wall. I stopped telling because it got to the point that whether I told or not, he would beat me up.

For me, this type of behavior almost became normal. It was not something I liked at all, but it was what I knew, and unfortunately expected. It seemed that being taunted by my brother became routine. If my brother didn't hassle me I wondered what was wrong. I got so used to the negative attention.

Aside from upsetting me, my brother's two favorite activities with me were wrestling and boxing. One night my mother was talking on the phone in the kitchen and preparing dinner. My brother wanted to box and I didn't feel like being his human punching bag again.

"No, I'm not boxing with you tonight," I said.

"If you don't box, I'll punch you in the face!" he demanded.

Based on my previous experiences I knew that he meant it, but I was so tired of giving in to him. I was hoping he was having a good day so that he'd leave me alone.

"Well, you'll have to punch me in the face because I am not letting you bully me around anymore," I said.

"Then you better guard yourself!" he said.

"Leave me alone," I pleaded.

"You better put your hands up, because I'm going to hit you!" he taunted.

I looked up and saw his fist coming toward my face and put my arms up, but he went under my arms and hit me right in my face. He purposely punched me; it was no accident.

As I began to cry, he told me to shut up and if I told, he would beat me up. I didn't think it made a difference if I cried or not, because he was going to have his own way no matter what. My eye and nose began to swell and ran crying into the kitchen to my mother.

"How did you get that black eye?" my mother asked.

"He hit me," I said.

"Did you hit your sister?" she asked.

My brother made up a story. I told my mother that he was lying about what happened and he knew what he was doing.

One night that week my mother went to a recovery meeting for alcoholics. I was ironing and my brother was walking around in his underwear calling me names. He jumped in my face and yelled at me. I took the iron close to him and told him that I'd burn his chest if he didn't leave me alone. He frowned at me and walked away. There were times that I felt something snapped in my head.

Wresting Gone Too Far

In the summer of 1979, my brother who was 12 at the time, moved in with my father to Illinois. I was so relieved when he left, because I knew his days of bullying me were over, but at the same time I missed him. We kept in touch by writing letters and sending conversations on cassettes to each other.

Looking for a fresh start, in March of 1980, my mother decided that we would move to Massachusetts to live with her sister, my Aunt Lulu. My mother and I moved when I was 11 years old and in 5th grade.

My brother had been gone almost a year when he decided that he wanted to leave Illinois and move with us to Massachusetts. It was great to see him, he seemed different, but within a few days he was back to his mischievous ways. He quickly began bullying and pushing me around, just as he had done a year ago before he moved away.

One night my brother wanted to wrestle while we were downstairs in the basement. He wrestled me to the ground, flipped me over and within seconds pinned me. This went on a few times. Then when he pinned me again, he didn't get up. I was uncomfortable and told him to get off me and he did. He told me it was some kind of new move.

One evening while we were watching television my brother came in the living room telling my mother that he wanted to show her a new wrestling move. So of course I was the contender and he wrestled me to the floor and pinned me just as he had done previously. He stayed on top of me until my mother yelled at him.

"Get off your sister and leave her alone," my mother yelled.

"It's a new move," he said.

My mother was at a recovery meeting and my aunt was out at the mall. My brother wanted to wrestle and told me to come down to the basement for a match. He started to wrestle me to the ground as he had done for the last week. When he pinned me to the ground, he didn't get up. I told him to get off me, but he didn't say anything. I started feeling movement. I started to shove him off but he held me down. I was uncomfortable and told him to get off, but he didn't.

"Stop and get off me!" I yelled as I pushed at him.

He got up and was mad at me.

"You're stupid anyway!" he said.

"If you tell mom I'll kick your face in," he said as he punched me and walked away.

I didn't think I did anything wrong. I was hurt and couldn't understand what just happened. *Why are you mad at me? You are the one acting weird, not me.*

One night my aunt and mother left the house and told us they would be back in a few hours. This was the night that my brother's 'wrestling' had gone too far.

We were in the basement and he pinned me to the ground but never got off me. I told him to get off me just as I had before.

"Get off me. Leave me alone," I begged him.

"No. Mom isn't here so I can do what I want to," he said.

That night my brother forced me to have sex with him. For the next several months any time my mother and aunt left the house, my brother would force me to have sex with him and perform other sexual acts. He told me if I told anyone that he would beat me up and that things would be harder for me. Every time he forced me to do something, I told him to stop. I yelled at him. I pushed him. I pleaded with him. However, it never helped. I was terrified of him, as every time he said he would hurt me, he did. I knew my brother didn't make threats; he made promises.

My brother hurt me whether I did what he wanted or not. I never won at his sick game. I was afraid of him and I thought it would only get worse so I never said anything. I always made sure he knew that I hated him. As the months passed, I felt powerless with him.

I remember times where I removed myself from what was happening, it was as if I was watching from a distance. When I was alone, I would yell at myself in the mirror and punch myself in the head and legs.

As the summer of 1980 approached, my mother decided that we would move back to New Jersey. When we moved back to New Jersey, my brother decided to move back to Illinois with my father. And once again I was relieved, although now my relief was for different reasons than before. *Yes, go, leave, thank you!*

Once my brother moved back to Illinois, I thought that was the end of my brother hurting me. I was happy that he was gone.

Summers In Maine

My grandparents owned two cabins in the woods of Maine and every summer since I was 4 years old, my family would go and visit for the summer. In the summer of 1980, I went to Maine and within a few weeks, my father flew my brother out to Maine to visit. The abuse continued while we were in Maine visiting my grandparents.

One afternoon he brought me into the woods and when he was done, I cried.

"What's your problem?"

I cried and stared at him and reached for my clothes.

"You act like I just raped you or something."

"Well, you just did!"

"You are so dramatic."

"I hate you! I hate what you do to me!"

"Whatever," he said as he walked away.

The mind games were astonishing. Half the time I didn't know what was going on. What hurt me and was really confusing to me was that my family would treat my brother so nicely. Even though I kept quiet about the sexual abuse, it was obvious that he was a bully, but for some reason his behavior was tolerated.

When I was 12 years old, I started to have many negative thoughts about hurting myself. I didn't understand why I was thinking these thoughts. I didn't want to die. I thought I deserved to feel some sort of pain or punishment and wanted to reprimand myself in some way.

During the summer of 1981 we went to Maine again and my brother came out and it continued a few more times. Within a couple weeks of being there, I had gotten my period for the first time; I was just shy of 13 years old. I was so happy.

I wasn't happy so much that I got my period, as I was that I knew what it meant. I was ecstatic because I knew that when you have your period that means you could get pregnant, and knew that the days of my brother forcing me to have sex with him were OVER! I had this courage and strength and ran to my brother and yelled in his face. This brought me new courage that I hadn't had before. I do realize that he could have continued, but he didn't. I told my brother that he couldn't do it to me anymore. He made me do other things to him, but after he moved back to Illinois, it never happened again.

Something Never Discussed

Over the next few years, I only saw my brother a few times as he remained living in Illinois with my father. For years I blocked out the abuse and tried to deal with what was before me.

As years passed and I grew older, I saw a lot of enabling in my family and a lot of things were tolerated. I had always felt like I was the one who was wrong and that it was my fault. I always battled with this. When someone does something wrong, shouldn't they be punished?

This was something my family never discussed, and me hating my brother was not permitted. I was told that I was wrong for hating my brother. I was so confused; he beat me up, raped me, and I was supposed to 'act natural'. It wasn't like he stole my candy bar or hit me once, this was over a long span of time, and this was not an isolated incident; it happened over and over again. I had the impression that most of my family members thought my brother was wonderful and felt that I couldn't tell anyone as I feared what they would think of me.

You Have Nothing To Be Guilty Of!

Let's talk guilt: Guilt is something that will eat away at you if you let it. You have nothing to feel guilty for. You were 10. It was not your fault. You were the child. You were a victim.

For me, I had many people try and throw the guilt rope at me, and if I grabbed it, I would have used it to hang myself. I think people point fingers at the victim because they think somehow you could have or should have done something to prevent it. People may also point fingers, because it gets the focus off of them and their potential responsibility. For example, although my parents were not involved or aware of the abuse with my brother, to me there were obvious clues that something was going on. Although the sexual abuse occurred in secret, my brother was visibly abusive, both physically and verbally. I believe for whatever reason that they chose to ignore it.

The bottom line is that guilt is remorse for feeling responsible for some offense. You didn't do anything wrong. You certainly did not deserve to be abused. Let go of the guilt.

Whatever abuse you went through is terrible, but know that it is over and you cannot be hurt in that way again. No, it was not God's will—God doesn't cause or make people rape, abuse, or hurt others. I don't have the answers for whatever happened to you, but what I can tell you is that it is over and you have hope and a future ahead.

You Have Nothing To Be Guilty Of!

CHAPTER 5

THROUGH THE YEARS

This was the first week at high school—it's different than I thought. Everyone from junior high seems like they are trying to fit in the crowd. All the girls I hung out with are more interested in the jock guys and dates than anything else. I think my best friend Shannon and I are starting to drift from each other. She's changing. I know I am not the same either, but why can't things stay the same? Why do things have to change so much?
Why? When things are going good, they change!
Journal entry – September of 1983

Who I Am

During high school I felt all torn up inside. I didn't know which end was up. I was overwhelmed with horrific thoughts and flashbacks. I couldn't focus in school and adapting to any kind of change seemed unattainable. I was extremely confused on my sexuality. Not only was I attracted to girls, but also I felt like I was a boy trapped in the body of a girl. I didn't want to be a girl at all. I felt awkward inside, but thought I was able to make people believe I was ok. I tried to hide my appearance by dressing in baggy clothes and suits. I liked that a person couldn't make out if I was male or female.

My best friend Shannon was amazing and understanding with me. Although I didn't confide in her about any abuse, she was supportive of me and tried to help me with the things I was going through. Although we were complete opposites, no matter what weird thing I was experiencing, she was right there with me. She had it together and always seemed to have a solution to everything. In the middle of freshman year she told me that her parents were looking to move to Brick, New Jersey. When she moved at the end of my freshman year, I didn't know what to do. I depended on her greatly. Although we talked on the phone and saw each other from time to time, we didn't see each every day like I was accustomed to.

Things Piling Up

Throughout the years I felt like no one would understood what I was feeling and began talking to myself and had conversations with my dog, Dolly. It was my desperate attempts of trying to figure out my life. Even though I realize she couldn't understand a word, I felt like someone was listening.

I began taking chunks of hair from my scalp. I would either cut it with scissors or take a razor close to my scalp. The first time my mother noticed that I had hair missing, she didn't know what to do or think. One afternoon, my mother and a friend of mine went out to the mall shopping and I took my hat off. I had several pieces of hair missing from my head. My mother walked ahead of us and when I would talk with her she would act as if she didn't know me. When we got home she was very upset and talked with me.

"Are you aware that people were staring at you?" she asked.

"No, I didn't really notice," I said sadly.

"People were staring and gawking at you."

"Oh".

"They were staring at you because you have pieces of hair missing from your head."

"Oh."

"I am ashamed to be seen with you."

"I'm sorry."

At that moment I was filled with remorse that I shamed my mother in such a way. I didn't mean to look like a freak. I didn't mean to upset her. From that point I constantly wore hats and my mother would randomly check my head to see if I had any new spots. She didn't know what was wrong and attributed it to growing pains and to awkward teenage years.

When I was 15 years old my mother noticed that I was having difficulties and took me to a therapist, who I called Dr. Bob. He told me that whatever I told him would be confidential and wouldn't tell my mother. I shared with him what happened with my brother, and as promised he didn't tell my mother.

Dr. Bob asked me various questions regarding my sexuality and wanted to know if I was gay. I told him that I was only interested in being with a girl if I could be a boy. I continued to talk with Dr. Bob on a weekly basis for a year despite the fact that he didn't help.

By the end of my sophomore year, June of 1985, I had accumulated appalling grades to where I would not graduate to the next year. I failed 5 out of 8 classes and the other grades were barely passing.

A few weeks later my mother got remarried. I refused to attend the wedding and reception because I didn't like the man or agree with her remarrying. I stayed with my grandmother for the next few weeks. I reluctantly moved in with my mother, her new husband, and his two daughters. I was dealing with many mixed emotions and was having conflict with my mother. By the end of the summer, my mother kicked me out of the house, and I went to live with my father in Illinois. About half way through, I missed my mother and moved back to New Jersey.

My Brother Returned

Shortly after moving back, my mother mentioned to me that my brother, who was now 19 years old, wanted to move in with us. Immediately I felt my heart racing. I was so upset I could scream. I didn't want him to live there, but I felt that I couldn't tell her why. There wasn't anything I could do about it.

Within a few weeks he started slapping me around. I told him that he was not going to mess with me anymore. He started calling me names and I walked over and told him that I was not his punching bag anymore. I felt anger boiling inside me. He pushed me and within seconds I snapped. I punched him in the shoulder and threw him up against the wall. I yelled in his face that I hated what he did to me and that he will never touch me again. I was so tired of him getting his way all the time. I warned him to stay away from me. Unfortunately, I never had the last word; he punched me in the stomach and walked away.

Every night for the next few weeks I found myself having flashbacks of the sexual abuse. When I would awake it appeared so real. It was as if I was reliving everything he had done to me. At the time, I had a stepsister who was 12 years old, which was around the same age the sexual abuse took place with me. I grew concerned that he may do it to her.

I thought I was going to hold onto this secret until the day I died. However, as the days progressed I couldn't hold it in any longer. I was going to burst if I didn't say anything. On the evening before Mother's Day I told my mother what my brother had done to me for years. She said she had no idea. I kept silent for way too long—it had been 6 years since the sexual abuse first began.

Later that day my brother called on the phone.

"I told mom what you did to me for years. I told her everything, you jerk!" I said.

"Vicki, why it's all over?" he said.

"It might be all over for you, but it's not over for me. I don't want you to ever do this again," I warned him.

When my brother got home, my mother talked with him and he admitted what he did but seemed unmoved, hard-hearted, and emotionless. My stepfather took my brother to talk to him and then my mother spoke with him. She explained to him that I was very upset and suggested he talk with me and let me scream, cry, yell, and get it out. He appeared unaffected and when she finished talking, she suggested that my brother and I go for a walk on the beach. I looked at her as if she was a lunatic. I thought that was one of the most ridiculous things I had heard and I walked away. I was astonished at my mother's reaction as I felt that his behavior was condoned, as he didn't receive any punishment. Nothing.

I dealt with many feelings and emotions and tried to hide what I was going through, I was torn up on the inside. Not only could I not understand what my brother did to me, but why. I was very confused.

Senior Year

My issues were piling up inside, and not before too long did my mother and I bump heads. One afternoon my mother and I got into an argument, she tore up my paycheck from work and I swore at her.

By the middle of August 1986, tension thickened between my mother and I. She kicked me out of the house for the second time. I moved back to Illinois to live with my father where I started my senior year of high school.

I had few friends but many acquaintances. I appeared to

be very outgoing; however, I felt horrible inside. I appeared confident, but was actually very insecure. Every day was a battle in my mind. I was contending with thoughts that were consuming me. When I would get home, I would punch myself in the face, legs, stomach, arms, but the relief seemed only to last a few moments.

One afternoon after school when I was 18 years old, I went home and had a brief discussion with my father. I yelled at him and ran up the stairs and he called after me. I ignored him and ran into my bedroom. I slammed the door and locked it. It seemed as if instantly things changed. I started hearing strange sounds and voices—there wasn't anyone around except for me. Suddenly I felt trapped. I heard shouts and screams inside my head. I felt an urgency to leave the house and didn't know where to go. I looked out the window to see if I could escape, but the jump to the ground was too far. I became extremely frightened.

I looked into the mirror and tried talking sense to myself. As I talked I noticed the metal braces on my teeth. *Take your braces off.* I looked for something to pry them off and found a pair of pliers in my room. I began to yank at my braces with the pliers and finally removed them. For a few minutes, after I yanked off the braces, I felt calm. Within minutes I became agitated and the voices were getting stronger. I went under my bed to get away from them; however, it didn't get better. I began talking to the voices I heard. Although I talked to myself for years prior to this, these were voices I could actually hear. I continued hearing voices through my adult years.

My mother told me a few years ago that as she looked back, the way I acted was not normal behavior. "I thought you were just going through a phase, and the hormones were kicking in. I was naïve in my thoughts. I believed that children were survivors and would get through whatever they faced, like they will bounce back. I was clueless, as I never have to deal with all the things you experienced. As years went on, you had so much hatred toward your brother and resentment to me. You thought you were right to hate him and expected me to hate him as well. You would get so upset seeing pictures of him."

Love Conquers Hate!

Raping another person is not normal, it is not right, it is wrong! I had so much confusion in my head about my brother. By him doing this to me, did this mean he hated me? Did this mean that I deserved what he did? I didn't understand and no matter what I did he would hurt me. I despised what my brother did and as years progressed it turned into hate. I hated my brother with a deep hatred. I thought my feelings were justified. I never thought forgiving him would be possible.

As I mentioned in Chapter 3, forgiveness is a key to healing emotionally and mentally. I have come to the conclusion that it is **better to love** than to hate. I don't at all condone what my brother did, I truly hate the acts that he did; however, hatred is not the answer and nothing good comes out of hatred. I forgave my brother in the summer of 1996 and saw him for the first time in 6 years. I told him that I forgave him of everything that he did and that I loved him. He seemed unchanged, but I had peace in my mind and heart that things were made right. That was the last time I saw or spoke with my brother. He took his own life in January of 2001.

There is something about forgiveness—it is freedom. It is letting go of the past and letting go of what should have been or could have been. When you act in love, you are winning.

Hate is an emotion that if not careful, can overtake you. You may find yourself consumed with things because you are driven by hate. By hating, you will only hurt yourself. Let loose of the grip you have clenched your hands so tightly on. Get ready for a new day!

Love does not think any evil thing, love does not rejoice when something terrible happens to someone, love doesn't behave crudely or abruptly, love is not conceited, and love is not easily angered.

Love is forgiving. Love is kind and unwearied. Love rejoices in the truth. Love endures. Love never ceases.

"And now abide in faith, hope, love, these three;
but the greatest of these is love."
The Bible, Book of 1 Corinthians,
Chapter 13, verse 13

CHAPTER 6

AN UPHILL BATTLE

*I'm enjoying boot camp. And, for the first time I feel like I
am good at something. It doesn't matter how feminine I am
or how I look because everyone here dresses and looks the
same. I can finally relax and not worry what people think
about me. This is the type of thing I was made for.
I can get dirty and it just doesn't matter.
I know I am going to do well here. I just know it.
An excerpt from a letter to my grandmother
– September of 1987*

In the USMC

I graduated high school in June of 1987 and headed back
to New Jersey for the summer. I joined the United States
Marine Corp on September 8, 1987, just a few days prior to
my 19th birthday.

While I was in boot camp, I developed Anorexia and
Bulimia. It didn't matter how much weight I lost because
when I reached that goal, I set another goal. I wasn't satis-
fied with the results that I attained. Eventually the word
got out and I was required to talk to a psychiatrist. After

speaking with the doctor and undergoing an evaluation, he offered me a medical discharge. I panicked. *No way! How could they discharge me, I am so good at this. What will I do if I am not here?*

"You have gone through a lot and eventually it will catch up with you," he said.

"What, what are you talking about?" I asked.

"I am not sure how stable you are. With this kind of thing on your side, you are going to end up taking medication for the rest of your life," the psychiatrist said.

"How can you say that? You are reading a chart. You don't even know me well enough to say something like that," I said.

"I am just telling you what I see," he shrugged his shoulders and grinned at me.

"Look, I can't get discharged. I'm actually good at this thing." I pleaded with him. I started to cry. *You can't cry in front of him, you will look weak. Stop crying.*

He told me he would give my superiors his recommendation along with my desire to stay in and attempt to complete boot camp. I got several commendations from various levels of leadership to continue. I was put on a trial basis to see how I'd do.

I was monitored day and night and although I struggled through all 13 weeks of boot camp, I managed to graduate in December of 1987.

After boot camp I was forwarded to Meridian, Mississippi for my training in aviation administration. I continued to battle with an eating disorder; however, I became discreet in eating and secretive in exercising. I made many friends at aviation school; nevertheless I kept what I was going through a secret. During the day I over exercised, minimized my food intake, and began to drink heavily every night. Not before too long I ended up in the hospital as a result of malnutrition. Upon release from the hospital, I was assigned to see a psychiatrist and a medical doctor twice a week to monitor my condition. I struggled through training; however, I finally graduated on March 4, 1988.

Below is from consultation notes, Meridian, Mississippi:

The patient is a 19-year-old white female in active duty, referred from the clinic for evaluation of malnutrition. The patient received temporary therapy while in boot camp. She denies previous psychiatric counseling. Denies any other pertinent history. Examination on admission revealed a weak appearing white female who appeared dehydrated. In view of this, she was admitted for more aggressive evaluation and therapy. The patient was admitted to the hospital, started on intravenous, multivitamins and initially placed on a liquid diet. She was placed in stress management group and went to daily group therapy sessions. I have tried patient on various food substances with little or no success. The case was discussed with USMC, and they planned on discharging her to a long-term treatment facility. The patient's superiors requested her release from hospitalization so that a psychiatrist on an outpatient basis may see her. Hospital Summary, February 4 – February 11, 1988

Alone In Mississippi

I had a week leave before I was due to arrive at my final duty station, Camp Pendleton, California. I had the option of flying back to New Jersey to visit my mother and grandmother or to visit my aunt Lulu and uncle Boris who lived in Mississippi. I had lost so much weight and didn't want my mother to worry, so I visited my aunt and uncle.

When I arrived at my aunt Lulu's house, she told me that my grandmother had gotten very sick and was in the hospital, and that she was flying out to New Jersey to see her. I went with my uncle to drive my aunt to the airport. Upon her departure, my uncle made dinner. He brought two tray tables with food and drinks and we sat on the couch and watched a game show. He placed his arm around me and said it was nice to have time together. Then he put his hand on my thigh. I was never close with my uncle, so it was very odd that he was touching me. I asked him what he was doing and he looked at me strangely. He told me to relax.

I was getting dizzy and the room appeared as if it was spinning. I turned to him and told him that I wasn't feeling well and that I was a little week and dizzy. I'm not quite sure if he put something in the food or if I had a reaction to something, but I think he drugged my food.

My uncle was a large and burly man, about 6' 5" and nearly 400 pounds. He picked me up and carried me into his bedroom. I told him to let me down. I yelled as loud as I could. Then he raped me.

The next morning when I got up he told me to sit down for breakfast. He made many sarcastic and degrading comments to me. He told me he was happy we were alone and had time together. He began describing what he did to me the night before and told me he was going to do it again.

"Why aren't you eating?" he asked.

"I lost my appetite," I mumbled.

He told me that he was leaving for work and that I was not to leave the house. As he was getting ready to walk out the door, he told me that I was not to use the telephone to call anyone and I was not to answer it if it rang. He said that he would know if I used the phone or if I left the house. I stayed in the house and cried most of the day.

Oh no, what am I going to do? I can't call anyone because he will know.

I was trapped in a house with someone who I thought was my uncle who was to care for me and look out for me. This was not the case.

Two days later he raped me again. It was worse than the first time.

Even though he told me not to tell anyone, he told me that if I said anything to anyone, they would not believe me. Then he quickly said that in the remote chance that they did believe me, he would say that I was just a troubled girl. He told me that I would look like a liar and it would be in my best interest if I kept my mouth shut.

That week was one of the worse weeks of my life. What he did was warped, demented, as well as disgusting and vile.

Escaping with Men

Throughout my time in the USMC I dated several men, a few women, and had several one night encounters. Although I wasn't attracted to men, I wasn't able to openly date women and I didn't want to get caught. Even though I wanted absolutely no sexual involvement, I went through with it as I thought it was one of my requirements. I thought I was supposed to have sex with a guy so I would. I desperately wanted to be loved and I thought that having sex would do it. It never did. It only added to my insecurities. Although most of the guys didn't leave me after sex, I would end the relationship with them.

Discharged from USMC

Upon my arrival to my duty station at Camp Pendleton, California, I was advised by my superiors to go see the doctor on base. I was evaluated and given a physical to monitor my progress and the status of my eating disorder.

Below is from consultation notes, Camp Pendleton, California:

Psychological testing revealed that the patient has an underlying characterolgical disorder with histrionic features of which the eating disorder is part of. The patient suffers from a longstanding disturbance of behavior and character of which the eating problem is a component. Her personality disorder will significantly impair her ability to adequately function in the USMC. She will benefit from outpatient therapy following discharge due to the need for long-term psychotherapy. Although she is not suicidal or homicidal, the patient should be considered a risk to herself if not separated.

Consultation Summary – May 3, 1988

I became an emotional rollercoaster. One day I was up thinking I would get better and the next day I crashed and thought there was no hope at all. I felt the only thing I could control was my body. Although I was under doctor supervision, I ended up in a hospital with severe malnutrition.

Below is from consultation notes, Camp Pendleton, California:

This is the patient's third psychiatric evaluation since enlistment. The patient was recommended for separation prior to completing recruit training, and recommended for separation last month by this clinician. Since her last evaluation, her symptoms have intensified resulting in dehydration and need for inpatient hospitalization. The patient maintained that she could not perceive the seriousness of her behavior in regard to not eating. Her affect was inconsistent when discussing her eating behavior. She seemed aloof to the consequences of her actions. Judgment was poor and immature and insight was limited. Diagnosis: Eating Disorder NOS and Mixed Personality Disorder with Dependent and Histrionic Features. Patient is unfit for duty. Recommend separation due to the severity of her disorder, which significantly impairs her ability to function effectively in the USMC.

Consultation Summary – June 1 through June 4, 1988

I didn't like the idea of quitting something, but I didn't

know what else to do; I felt trapped. I felt that if I stayed in the USMC, life would become worse.

Within days of my one-year anniversary, I was discharged with an honorable/medical discharge. I moved from California to Chicago and then within months, back to New Jersey into a small cottage owned by an old family friend.

Focus On The Task At Hand

My main focus was trying to figure out what was going on in my body. It seemed that the one and only thing that I was in control of was my body; I had total control of what went into it. I couldn't control any person, or any situation, but I could definitely control my body. By not eating I thought that I had complete control. I used to have a saying, 'Anorexia doesn't have control over me—I have control over it.' I began a vicious cycle of exercise and binging, then exercise and minimal eating to eventually no food intake.

I felt such strength and energy, it seemed that as the days went on, the more in 'control' I became. I was focused. I would run in the cold of the winter for miles, and then exercise for another hour. Although I began eating, I continued to throw up and use laxatives 2-3 times a day. I battled with an eating disorder for several years following and did a fairly good job of hiding it from others.

I made so many poor choices based on my past. One poor decision snowballed into another.

Make Good Choices!

The choices you make today will result in your tomorrow. Think about it for a moment: Good choices equal high-quality results and bad choices equal terrible results.

Think about some choices:
- Yes **OR** No
- Good **OR** Bad
- Love **OR** Hate

- Success **OR** Failure
- Heaven **OR** Hell

It is not necessarily all black and white, but if you 'stand in the middle' then you are accepting mediocre. It's like having one foot in the door and one foot out—you know what you should do, but you don't do that (good choice) because you fear, you dread, etc.

Here are some things that may result in the choice you make:
- Thinking on something good **OR** thinking on something bad
- Asking for help **OR** hiding in secret
- Becoming hopeful and open to change **OR** thinking things will never change
- Coming forward about a horrifying incident **OR** keeping quiet out of fear
- Taking a step away from a crisis **OR** acting out on emotions

There are so many varieties of things to choose from. There is always a multiple of choices—we can pick and choose what we want to do.
Make Good Choices today!

CHAPTER 7

ACTING ON EMOTIONS

Another therapy session! Oh, how I hate therapy. Therapy is like throw-up. Think about it—Each time I go to therapy, I spill my guts onto the table and pick at each little part—a little here and a little there. Rather than talking about one thing at a time and dealing with it, I pick and poke at everything all at once. I'm staring at this big pile of throw up that stinks so badly. I'm dealing with it and moving on. What is therapy doing for me anyway? I'm afraid of the past. I don't like talking about it. When I do talk about it, bad things happen, I never felt better about myself.
Journal entry – winter of 1991

Flashbacks Became My Reality

In the spring of 1988, I began going to gay clubs and parties. In the summer of 1989, a few days prior to my 21st birthday I met an attractive woman, Dina, who was 7 years older than me. We began dating and six months later in March of 1990, I moved in with her. After being together for a year, I began to feel safe with her and told her of my abusive past. I had flashbacks throughout the years; however, they started to intensify where I began having terrible flash-backs and nightmares about my brother and my uncle. The flashbacks got so bad that I actually thought my uncle Boris was coming to kill me. I would see my uncle on my porch, in my car, and following me in the mall. I was terrified. I would call the house in Mississippi to make sure he was there and when he would answer I'd hang up. I wanted to make sure that he was home and I was safe. It was as if I was reliving the moment when he raped me.

It got so bad that Dina suggested that I talk with a thera-pist. I wasn't convinced that going to a therapist was a good idea as the therapists I had seen up to this point seemed unable to help me with my troubles. I never felt better after therapy, only worse.

Dina persuaded me to go to therapy, so I began counsel-ing with a therapist, Claire. I was not fond of her, but went anyway. When I was in therapy sessions, it would be as if I was reliving the situation over and over again, it seemed that my torment never ended.

Unable to Cope

After a few sessions of therapy with Claire, they became more intense. At one session I discussed the situation with my uncle and as I was in the middle of a sentence, she told me my time was up.

"Okay, your time is up," she said as she pointed to her watch.

"Huh?" I asked. I just looked at her in amazement.

"Your time, it is up. We will continue next week," she said.

Here my emotions were all over the place, and she didn't give me any time to wind down. I became incredibly angry. I was becoming enraged. I felt like I had just been raped all over again. I was yelling and screaming on the way home, then I pulled over and cried. I hit myself a few times, yelled at myself, then cried some more and then calmed down.

As I was driving home, a man in a small gray car cut me off and nearly hit an elderly woman as she crossed the street. Instantly I became infuriated. I flipped out and chased after this man throughout town. I was driving on the wrong side of the road, honking my horn, and yelling at him to pull over. He finally did pull over. I had all the hatred of my uncle and brother built up from my therapy session and I was ready to fight.

I got out of my car and ran over to his car and began pounding on the window.

"Get out of your car, you jerk!" I yelled.

As he got out of the car, I noticed he was well over 6 feet tall, but that didn't stop me from getting closer to him.

"What are you out of your mind?" he asked.

"No, you are out of your mind! You nearly hit that lady and you cut me off!" I yelled.

He looked at me up and down. I was wearing black jeans, a black leather jacket, boots, and black sunglasses and I had short dark hair.

"What are you a dyke or something?" he asked.

"What does that have to do with anything, you moron!" I exclaimed.

"Why else would you have chased me down?" he asked.

"Why? Because you are a jerk who cut me off and almost hit that old lady!" I yelled.

At that moment I was filled with so much anger. I got closer to him and punched him in the face. Much to my surprise, he punched me right back.

I fell back onto my truck and looked at him in shock and unbelief.

"You weren't supposed to hit me back!" I yelled.

The man ran to his car. I began trembling. I walked to my truck, crying and wiping the blood from my nose. I was devastated.

As he drove past me, he stuck up his middle finger. I got angry all over again. As he took off, I quickly got into my truck and went after him, but he vanished. I never saw him again.

When I got home my countenance changed from anger to sadness. I didn't understand what had taken place. I was distraught. This was the first time I had ever been called a dyke and it bothered me.

Dina had taken the day off to spend with me and was surprised when I came home with a bloody nose and black eye. After that session, Dina called and scheduled a new therapist for me.

Being Honest

I continued with a new therapist, and after a few months she was moving. I was reluctant to start all over again with another therapist, but I did. I met Jan and I seemed to like her from the start. She seemed caring and nice, and she actually seemed interested in helping me. We talked about my abusive past, my poor choice in coping mechanisms, my unhealthy relationships, and my need to fit in. She tried to get me to focus on being honest with myself and talk about things when I was upset. She suggested that I begin to write in a journal. It was partly a good idea and partly a bad idea. Writing allowed me to express myself and get my thoughts out; however, I didn't know how to separate the past from the present and would 'relive' the situations I had gone through.

In the fall of 1991, I finally told my mother about my uncle raping me years before. Unfortunately, she was not as supportive as I imagined she would be, but in her defense, I think she was shocked. What really upset me was that she wanted to know details. I kept quiet about what my uncle had done for 4 years. I lived in fear from the words he said. Although I was terrified of him, I've since realized that his words were just a bunch of sounds with hot air.

In 1997 I forgave my uncle for raping me. I made a choice to forgive him.

The Move That Changed Me

On September 8, 1992 I was given a promotion and transferred to a store 4 hours from where I lived. I was told that this was the best for my career and the ultimate career move. I believed it and I thought that my whole life revolved around this job. I had the notion that if I didn't take this job; my life would be over.

Instantly my life changed. I was miserable. Dina was very disappointed that I took a job without talking with her. Soon she and I weren't doing well.

The one thing that I stood on, other than the job, was Dina. I basically believed all she said, and when she said we could get through anything, I was convinced of it. For the next three months I traveled back and forth from Connecticut to New Jersey and Dina did the same.

When I first arrived at the store, I became friendly with one of the store managers in the mall, Lynette. We had lunches a few times and started being a little friendlier.

"I want you to know that I don't like you the way you may think, and I don't want to be with you in any romantic kind of way. I just want to be friends," Lynette said.

I actually thought this was funny, because I had not even thought of her in that way. "Okay, Lynette, now don't hold back, please tell me what is really on your mind," I said sarcastically.

I smiled and we both laughed. She was so straightforward with me and I liked her honesty. She was truthful to me and didn't hide anything from me. Over the months we quickly became close friends.

In December of 1992, the traveling back and forth took a toll on my relationship with Dina. A few days before Christmas, our relationship came to an end. I thought Dina was all I had and this broke me. The rejection I was feeling was unbearable. I couldn't deal with it and it turned my life upside down.

The only way I could block out my feelings was by staying busy. After we broke up, I dedicated all my time toward work. I worked anywhere from 60 to 80 hours a week.

I couldn't deal with all the emotions I was feeling. I wanted to be an ostrich and bury my head in the sand in hopes that everything would just get better somehow. The realization came that I was alone and far from anyone I knew. During this time I began to drink on a daily basis. I took speed during the day to compete with crazy retail hours and drank at night. I would drink until I passed out.

One night I was extremely frustrated and was feeling out of control. I felt like I wanted to hurt myself. I started talking to myself and looked at myself in the mirror. I took a nail clipper and broke off half of my front tooth.

In January of 1993 I found out that Dina was seeing someone. This turned me into a tailspin. I couldn't eat or sleep. I started doing drugs and going out to clubs almost every night.

Cutting the Pain

Things were intensifying for me and I was doing everything I could to escape from the internal pain I felt every waking hour. In March of 1993, two women, Lia and Kary befriended me. Lynette warned me that they were manipulative and deceitful; however, I didn't see it. Neither of them ever had money and we'd go out and I would pay for both. I had them over for dinner and they asked me if I could have one wish come true what would it be. I didn't respond. Then they asked if I wanted to ever have a sexual experience with two other women. I looked away and didn't answer.

On May 1, of 1993 Lia and Kary had come over and they were going to spend the weekend at my studio apartment.

My apartment was entirely open and there were no walls. I went to sit on my couch and turned around and saw them on my bed. They were in my bed together and I never felt so alone. Suddenly things were piling up in my mind. Then, it finally hit me that my friend Lynette was right about them. They didn't care about me, and they just wanted a place for themselves. I had two people over who I thought liked me and they didn't even act like they cared unless I was doing something for them.

Get a knife. Cut yourself. Instantly I felt alone and I casually went into the kitchen and grabbed a butcher knife. I walked outside to the porch and for the first time I cut myself. I began to cut at my wrist. I was numb from drinking and although I didn't feel any pain, I started crying as the memories of the last year were flooding my mind. The more I thought, the more I felt like I was losing everything. *You can't get me. You can't hurt me. Go away. No, make it stop, make the pain go away...please just stop!* I stopped cutting and went to take a shower and they were still in my bed. I came out of the bathroom and they were still there. I got some more rum and just lay on the kitchen floor and cut my left wrist some more. They called the police and told them that I tried to kill myself. Shortly after the police were called, they arrived at my apartment along with an ambulance.

The police report as follows:

Attempted Suicide – On May 1, 1993 we spoke with the complainant, Kary Muper who said that her friend, Vicki tried to commit suicide by slicing her wrists with a knife. The wounds were superficial to her left wrist and several were done on other occasions. Vicki was transported to Waterbury Hospital by ambulance for observations. A police emergency examination test was ordered for Vicki. The knife was found on the porch and turned in as evidence. Kary Muper said that Vicki had been drinking a lot and did not realize that she was there. Vicki did not want to talk about the incident.

Police Department, Waterbury, Connecticut
— May 1, 1993

I was rushed to the hospital where I had a psychiatric evaluation. I don't remember trying to kill myself that night. I just remember wanting the pain to end. I wanted to have peace and consistency but didn't know exactly how to go about it.

The First Hospitalization
On May 1, 1993 I was admitted to Psychiatric Hospital in Waterbury, Connecticut. Below is from consultation notes:

The patient is an alert, calm, cooperative boyish looking 24 year old, casually dressed with good eye contact. The patient suffers from anorexia nervosa and frequency of induced vomiting and use of laxatives and suppositories increased in the past few months. Her mood was described as depressed and affect was consistent with the mood state. She had vague suicidal ideation and vague suicidal planning. She was looking at objects feeling like using them to hurt herself but she categorically denied any suicidal intent or plan or homicidal ideation, intent or plan. Her attention was easily aroused.

Psychiatric Hospital, Waterbury, Connecticut
— May 1, 1993

When I had awoken, I was uncertain where I was. I didn't have my clothes, I was in a gown and my hair was messed up.

It turns out that Lia and Kary took my clothes after I was admitted in the emergency room. They drove off in my truck, used my credit cards that were in my purse, and were staying at my apartment.

Dina was contacted and told that I was in the hospital. When Dina arrived, a doctor told her that they believed she was the reason I was there and advised her to leave. Dina immediately called my mother.

"Dina, what should I do? Should I go see her?" my mother asked.

"You should go see her," Dina said.

When my mother arrived for the first time, she was in shock. Years later when I asked her about that day, this is what she told me. "There are several instances with you that are traumatic that I would never want anyone to go through. When I walked into the hospital it was almost like an out of body experience. There were steel doors with a small window, and the grounds were fenced in. It was a very dark place. I couldn't believe I was seeing my daughter in an insane asylum. These things happen to other people not me. I was in shock and upset. You were on speed and always working so many hours. You were doing that to cover the hurt of your broken relationship. I didn't know how you were doing it. A lot of the instances you went through were overwhelming and I blocked a lot of it out of my mind."

The second day of my admission, my mother stopped by while Lia and Kary were visiting me. My mother told me that there was something about them that she didn't like. She said I was too sick to see the truth, so she called Lynette and Dina.

Lynette called the police and within the week, they confiscated the truck from Lia. Later on that day, Dina called them and told them to get out of my life. I never saw Lia or Kary again.

Continuous Thinking

My doctor told me that I lacked structure and part of being in the psychiatric unit was to establish structure in my life. My routine began with breakfast followed by a session of group therapy, an activity, lunch, then another session of group therapy, then a craft or activity, then dinner, group, then free time. Since the Marines I had not had any structure, and I started to like the routine.

Although I hadn't ever actually cut before this, I began to familiarize myself with anything that I could cause a cut with. *You can use knives and forks. Take them when no one is looking, they won't even notice they are gone.*

All throughout the hospital stay I thought about cutting that night and the immediate release it gave me. I kept thinking about the next time and was mesmerized with the thought of seeing the blood, getting a scar and feeling pain. I started thinking about what I would be able to do if I had sharp knives or razor blades. It may not have been the most positive, but to me it was the most effective way to get immediate results from the anguish I was experiencing on the inside. I started to think about what I wanted to do to my body. I became absorbed in getting a scar along with feeling pain. I decided I didn't want to scratch, as I felt that scratching wouldn't leave a scar. If I was going to spend time and effort doing this, there should at least be a noticeable mark from it. I wanted cuts that would scar so that it would match the pain and scars I had internally.

I took forks and hid them in different places in my room. Throughout the day I would clench one in my fist and punch it down firmly into my arm. I would watch the blood spurt out from the little puncture wounds. Within a day a bruise would develop from the punching.

Becoming More Destructive
The nurses looked at my arm and noticed that it hadn't been like that the day before and soon realized what I was doing. They told my doctor and I was given my first dose of medication. It seemed as though it was not working, I felt

completely out of control. And, I was not allowed to go out of sight of the nurse's station and had to tell them where I was going within the wing of the unit, as they feared that I would continue to hurt myself.

I was really annoyed, as this was my only outlet. I got so much relief. With this restriction it limited my ability to cut, so I started taking knives from other peoples dinner trays and forced them into my arm with all my strength. I would also take pens and pencils and jab them into my arm. These small accounts of harming were enough to curb my cravings until I could cut again. When the nurses would change my bandages they saw that there were fresh wounds and told my doctor.

When I had my visit with my doctor, he increased my medication and not only would I have the same restrictions within the wing, but also a nurse would have to go with me to the bathroom and during showers.

One afternoon we had arts and crafts and I was not allowed off the floor because I was on 'watch'. Since I was observed so carefully, it was difficult for me to get involved in activities. I wanted to leave the unit so that I could find something to hurt myself with. I asked one of the floater nurses if I could go to arts and crafts and she allowed me to go. I was making a wallet, and as everyone was looking at the crafts, I took a look at what supplies were around. I was looking for something sharp. To my dismay I didn't find anything sharp, only blunt objects. As I was making my wallet, I noticed that the plastic string I was using was very durable. *You could use that to hurt yourself, maybe even choke yourself. Maybe you could kill yourself.* I wrapped it around my hands and stretched it to see how durable it was. It seemed strong and since it didn't snap I figured I could use it later, so I grabbed a handful and shoved it into my pocket.

Why do you want to live? You don't. You can do this. You know you want to do this. You will be so much happier.

JUST DO IT! I had thoughts of dying and was convinced that if I wrapped the plastic string around my neck, I would be able to cut off my airway. When I got back to the psychiatric unit, I went into the bathroom, stood in front of the mirror and told myself that it was time to die. I wrapped the plastic string around each hand three times and around my neck five times. I tightly pulled on each side. I watched myself in the mirror as I turned from white, to red, then bluish purple. *Relief is on its way.* I began to get dizzy, and placed my back up against the wall and slid down to the floor. I barely heard knocking at the door. The next thing I remember was feeling a hand on my shoulder. I heard someone talking; however, it sounded gargled.

"What is going on here?" the nurse asked.

Her words echoed in my head. I was trying to open my eyes and focus. I looked up and noticed the nurse was standing over me. All I could get out was a whisper.

"Nothing is going on. I guess this means I'm not dead," I whispered.

Suddenly she let out a gasp as she noticed the plastic string around my neck. "Oh goodness, you've got something around your neck!" she exclaimed.

She struggled to free the string from my clenched fists and untangled all the string from around my neck.

"What were you trying to do?" she asked.

"Just trying to die, that's all," I whispered calmly.

The nurse removed the string from my neck and once I came to full consciousness, she asked, "Where did you get the string from?"

"From arts and crafts this afternoon," I answered.

When she walked out, I looked in the mirror. *You idiot, you can't even die right!*

Later on I asked the nurse why I didn't die. She said that when I pulled the string around my neck I passed out. When I passed out, I lost my grip to hold the string and it loosened up and I was able to breath.

My doctor was told of the situation and explained to me that he felt that I didn't have an understanding of my limitations. He believed that I could not control myself and increased my medication. I was restricted to a specific area of the ward and a nurse went with me to the bathroom and they watched me at night. There were some nights a nurse would have her chair right next to the door, just a few feet from my bed. It was at this point where I actually began to feel safe because I felt I was protected from myself.

Keep The Focus

During one of my sessions, the doctor stressed the importance of focusing on therapy. He explained it is important to focus on therapy and getting better rather than establishing new friendships and relationships. They figured that if you have new relationships going on, then you wouldn't try and fix the problem that is current.

One day my father had come up for a visit and wanted to speak with the doctor and nurses to see what type of arrangements he would need to make for me, and wanted to know what he could do for me. To my surprise, my father didn't know about any of the abuse that had taken place in my life. My father was very shocked because this was the first time he said he was ever told.

The day approached when I would soon be released from the psychiatric unit.

Along with the doctors, my family determined that it wouldn't be good for me to live alone. The doctors suggested I move in with someone who I was not too close with to avoid bringing up negative memories.

Discharge Summary:
During the hospital stay, the summary of treatment was as follows: Group Therapy, Medication, Individual therapy,

Educational Groups, Counseling, Behavior Modification, Antidepressants, and Psychotherapy.
> *Psychiatric Hospital, Waterbury, Connecticut*
> *– May 27, 1993*

Where Feelings May Lead You!

Almost all of the unhealthy things I did were a reaction to a feeling or an overwhelming emotion that I experienced. We are moved by our feelings. Major decisions are made by feelings.

A few examples of negative and positive feelings are as follows:

- Negative—rage, shame, irritation, anger, hatred, sorrow, or disappointment
- Positive—happiness, love, joy, or excitement

Feelings, especially the negative ones, can abruptly change based on circumstances. That is why it is important not to make decisions on feelings alone. The situation you are in is temporary. You don't want to make a permanent solution to a temporary problem. Feelings are fickle. They can be impulsive and unpredictable. They can be random and inconsistent.

It is okay to experience a negative feeling; it is how you react to the feeling that matters. If you are having a relatively good day and suddenly you get bad news or someone hurts your feelings, do you automatically turn into a state of confusion or think about doing something like harming?

Think about the last time you were angry, disappointed or hurt. How did you react? What actions followed your reaction? Think about the last time you were happy or content with a situation. How did you react? Were there any actions that followed?

When handled correctly, bad feelings are all right; however, if the feeling is overwhelming be careful in responding to it. If you react to the feeling without thinking through the possible repercussions of your actions, the outcome could be questionable.

However, when you think things through you can have a great result.

Remember to try to look at your circumstance in the best way possible!

CHAPTER 8

IN THE MIDST OF DESTRUCTION

*Mom, On Sunday night things didn't go well. I was really
upset and I flipped out. I just couldn't handle anything they
were talking about and I tore my room apart. I cracked up.
I threw my belongings around and broke my clock, hair
dryer, and I couldn't calm down. They gave me a tranquilizer and an anti- anxiety pill but before that, I couldn't talk
or even look at the people. I started packing up my stuff
because I don't feel like I belong anywhere, ever! I know I
don't handle change well and I cannot accept help
because I don't know how to receive it.
This is not making much sense. I'm done. See you soon.
Letter to my mother – June 26, 1993*

What I Was Becoming

As horrible as the sexual abuse was, the most horrific
part of my life was inflicted by myself. I view cutting
and burning myself as the worst thing—this was something
that I could have controlled and avoided altogether, as it was

something I did to myself by myself. I could not control the abuse that took place by others, but I could control what I did to myself.

The 'serious' self-injury began heavily in 1993 and lasted through the middle of 1995. The feelings I had were consuming and overtaking me. The vices intensified and the feelings were real. This is something that was overtaking me. There were times that I was calculating in my thinking, but overall it was something I was consumed with and was no longer something I did, it was who I became.

Cutting As A Way Of Life

My mother and therapist told me that I became preoccupied with cutting and they tried not to ask me too often if I cut. They said that I would become very tight lipped about it and refuse to talk about it.

The feeling to cut intensified and was consumed with thoughts of it. *I can go deeper, I can do more damage, and I can do it all.* I started cutting every time I sensed an uncontrollable thought. I started to cut if I got upset or if someone did something to me, real or imagined. It was like something nudging at me telling me that I wouldn't be able to relax unless I cut up a part of my body. The more I gouged into myself, it was as if I was experiencing a new freedom. When I cut, it gave me a release and sense of accomplishment and helped me deal with all that happened to me. I felt as if no one understood me and that cutting was my only way of escape. I never talked about it.

Although I took many psychiatric medications for my various disorders, it only helped for a while. Yes it helped for a while, but then it seemed like the effect 'wore off'. As much as I wanted out of the hospital I was afraid to be on my own. I had a difficult time moving forward. My future looked bleak.

This was horrific to people, but just a way of life for me.

There were many times where I woke up bloody and didn't remember what had occurred. It was the way I coped with the pain, the past, the present, and anything that was uncomfortable or unbearable to me.

Upon getting out of the hospital, my mother packed up my apartment and my father arrange for me to live with some relatives in New Jersey.

While I was at the house of my relatives, I felt out of place. It was not structured like the hospital, and I was alone most of the day. One night after dinner, my uncle gave me a lecture on responsibility. He mentioned that I was not a very good example for his children. He also told me that using any utensils in the house was off limits. He went on and on about how what I was doing was wrong.

As he was drinking his vodka straight up, I wondered if he had ever thought his kids could make up their own minds. I wasn't quite sure what to do.

After he had spoken to me in this manner, I was uncomfortable living there and felt utterly out of control. Even though he told me not to use any utensils in the house, I went to the kitchen pretending to help clean up. I opened the utility drawer and searched for the sharpest knife. I grabbed a knife and walked into the den. I took it into my hand and sliced up my arm. Once I saw a good amount of blood I stopped.

Out Of Control

The urges to cut were too strong for me to handle and I went out and bought a butcher knife and a paring knife and began alternating with slashing and stabbing. I used one for slashes and deep cuts, and the other for stabs. What I would carry out was always dependent on the frame of mind I was in. There were times that I would stop when I saw an immense amount of blood, and other times when I would continue cutting until I felt I cut deep enough. It all varied depending on where I was mentally. I was getting out of control again and was admitted to SC Psychiatric Unit on June 23, 1993.

Below is from consultation notes:

This is a 24 year old white single female who was admitted to SC Psychiatric Unit on June 23, 1993 because of depression, insomnia, anorexia, which has been going on for the past 6 months. While in this hospital, the patient cut her left arm reopening the wound that she had inflicted while at the hospital in Connecticut. The patient cut herself with the broken end of a metal spoon as she removed the rounded portion of the spoon so as to have a jagged sharp instrument. It is important to note that the patient had taken the spoon during her first day of hospitalization at this hospital and kept it hidden for the 'right time' in which to use it. So, although the patient is impulsive in her behavior, she is also quite calculating and planned to have 'impulsive episodes' in which she inflicts pain. The patient also has been noticed during the hospital at this time to be violent and has thrown objects during her treatment here.

I never was counseled on the self-harming aspect of it. It seemed that most therapists thought that was the least of my problems; if they could get beneath the cutting, they would find the real problem. Actually my whole life was the problem, I thought that was quite evident.

Acting On Every Impulse

I continued cutting every time I sensed an uncontrollable or uncomfortable thought. If I had a bad thought—I cut. A flashback—I cut. If someone hurt my feelings—I cut. If I had an anxiety attack—I cut. It became a reaction, a reactive impulse.

I initially hid the cuts from my mother. When cuts were exposed, she would ask what happened. Most of the time I avoided the question. One time I answered her and

told her my cat did it and she said, "Vicki, cats scratch—
they don't cut."

Each time I would cut myself and go to the hospital, I
was given a psychiatric evaluation. I learned very quickly
how to play the 'sane game' and stay out of the hospitals
and taught myself to stitch up my cuts.

One time I was driving to my mother's house and when I
arrived at her door my arm was covered in blood. When she
answered the door she was smiling and motioned to hug me.
Immediately the smile disappeared when she gasped and
looked at me and said, "Vicki, my God what happened to
you?" I looked over and the left sleeve of my white shirt was
full of blood. I didn't even know I cut myself. Apparently, I
sliced up my arm while driving down to her house. Later on
that day, I went to my truck and found a razor blade on the
floor under the glove compartment and another one inside
with bloody napkins. I have no recollection of that incident,
nor do I remember what triggered it.

I am not certain that I knew what I was doing to my
body was wrong. However, I do know that even though I
had a sense of peace afterwards, that was a false sense of
peace and security, because the same feelings to cut would
come back again and again. I then realized that causing self
inflicted pain and injuries to my body were not a good thing
and that nothing positive comes of it. I realized that cutting
my body was wrong, but I felt that I couldn't stop.

Back And Forth

Shortly after my stay at the psychiatric unit, it was
established that I needed help overcoming Anorexia and
Bulimia. I was admitted to an Eating Disorder Unit (EDU)
on July 6, 1993.

During a group session we talked about self-esteem and
it went into the pasts of other people and sexual abuse. One
of the girls was getting into such detail and was getting so

upset that as she was speaking, it appeared as if she was going through it all over again. It was as if she was reliving the incident. I was getting agitated and felt myself 'going away in my head'. It was very disturbing for me. I jumped up and ran out of the room and ran for the door. As I heard the nurses shouting, I just blocked them out and ran out the door.

Suddenly I sensed a drastic change and felt that I was not myself. I started walking real slow and headed out the door off the ward. I walked back and forth along the hallway dragging my knuckle across the brick wall. I saw two security guards coming toward me and just kept walking; it seemed as if everything was in slow motion. When they approached me, I heard voices, but could not make out what they were saying. The one guard placed his hand on my arm and I flinched, went to hit him, and took off running. I ran back to the unit and hid under the bed. I don't know if anyone knew I was there or not, I don't even know where I was. I guess things were really bad. I urinated on myself. I remember it happening, but it was as if I had no control over myself.

The next day, on July 20, 1993 I was given a psychiatric evaluation and discharged from EDU. I was sent back to the psychiatric unit and told my medication would be changed and I would come back once it was adjusted. It appeared as though medication was always the answer. I was given a pill that was used for certain psychiatric disorders, such as impulsive behavior; a pill which relieves nervousness and tension; a pill that was used to treat mental depression and insomnia; a pill that was used to treat symptoms of certain types of mental or emotional conditions; a tranquilizer, and a pill for anxiety attacks. I took 17 pills daily.

On August 2, 1993 I was sent back to EDU where I continued the inpatient program. In between group sessions, I was sitting on the couch across from another girl, Jo who was there for bulimia. From what I heard in the group sessions, she had a past with self-destructive behavior. I looked at her leg and she had carved 'LIFE SUCKS' into her left thigh.

"Why would you do that?" I asked

"To remind me that life does suck," she answered.

"Life doesn't suck all the time," I said, trying to be of some encouragement.

"Yes, it does suck all the time. Look at you," she said.

"What do you mean, 'look at me'?"

"Look at your arms, buddy," she said.

"Yeah, so that doesn't mean that I think life sucks. I just think what people did to me sucks and I don't know how to deal with it," I said sternly.

"Whatever." She shrugged her shoulders and went back to reading her magazine.

It is odd really; I thought that what she did was so peculiar even though I was in the midst of cutting myself. It was amazing that I could see trouble with others and view their actions as wrong, or destructive, but when it came to myself I couldn't see it. I really enjoyed helping others; though, I could never help myself.

Struggling

I was discharged from the inpatient program at EDU on September 2, 1993. I moved into a house in Clark, New Jersey as a boarder. I continued going to EDU in the outpatient program. I was there from 8:00 a.m. to 5:00 p.m. Monday through Friday. It was very structured with group sessions and a couple times a week, I would meet with my doctor.

I was taking my medication as prescribed; however, I was struggling to make things work. There were times I felt okay for a few hours. However, most of the times I couldn't handle my life. The flashbacks, the memories, the emotions, the thoughts, and the feelings of rejection were too much for me to handle.

I was just trying to cope with each day. I felt miserable on the inside. No matter what I tried to do, it never got better. No matter whom I dated, what I did, where I went, or the clothes I wore, nothing changed.

Throughout my years of counseling and hospitalizations, various therapists and doctors told me that I was more determined to hurt myself than I was to recovery. One doctor said, "You are so determined to cause harm to yourself. Why not put all that energy into helping yourself? If you put all that energy that you have invested into negative things and focus it on the positive, you will get well."

I remember thinking that it sounded good, but wasn't attainable by any stretch of the imagination. I couldn't accept the concept. It would require change and I just couldn't bear to think about that. I was convinced he was clueless on how to help me and ignored what he said.

The Same Yesterday – Today – Forever

I always hear people comment that they want things to stay the same and that they feel that everything in their life changes. "Things always seem to change, why can't things just stay the same?"

Think about it for a moment:
- **People change**—their attitudes, lifestyles, moods, minds
- **Circumstances change**—world events, governments, leaders, school   situations, home & life surroundings
- **Seasons change**—Summer, Spring, Winter, Fall

You may have things in your life that go up and down like a yo-yo, or you base your decisions on your current circumstances; there is always time to change. Change can be good—if it is for the good.

There is One who never changes, who is the same yesterday, today, and forever: God. He is unchanging, ever faithful and always around for you.

In this fast paced world, know that as much as things move and shake, there is One who is always there and never changing! People may change with the times and seasons, but God never will. He is always there for you!

"Jesus Christ is the same yesterday, today, and forever."
The Bible, Book of Hebrews, Chapter 13, verse 8

Have a life Changing time!

CHAPTER 9

MAKING A PERMANENT MARK

*Dear Mom, Hi. I know these past few months have not been
easy on you. I know you have been reaching out to me,
praying, driving 3 hours one way just to see me, cleaning
my disgusting apartment. I imagine the thought of your
daughter wanting to die is not a good one. You have been
working very hard as a mother to help me through the last
two hospitalizations. I have not been myself with
medications changing and new doctors. This hospital
stay is different. Believe me, a lot of emotions have been
stirred up inside of me more so being in this hospital.
I want it to work this time. Right when I get ready to quit, I
have to pick myself back up and I guess my point
is this: Even though you have not been in the hospitals the
last few months, you have had to work just as hard as I
have and I want to thank you for not giving up.
We can't give up. I say we, because one person
can't battle this pile of junk alone! I have no idea what the
future brings. All I know is that I am in a hospital
scared and I imagine it will all fall into place somehow.*

I appreciate all that you have tried and I love you.
Letter to my mother – summer of 1993

A Thought Acted Upon

One morning as I was driving to the EDU, I had a thought I never had before. *You need to burn yourself. Burn your forearm. Light it on fire.* All the way there I had these overwhelming thoughts to burn myself on my forearm. I arrived at EDU and tried to ignore the thoughts and figured they would go away. After leaving the EDU, I continued to have overwhelming thoughts to burn my forearm. I saw a picture of it in my mind. I remembered the owner of the house where I was a boarder telling me that she and her family would be away for the weekend. At that moment I decided it was time to make a large permanent mark that would never have the chance of fading away. I wanted people to see the pain I was feeling inside. I figured if my scars from cuts weren't doing it, that maybe a big blotch from a burn would. On the way to my room I stopped off to buy some beer, cigarettes, lighters, and a fire starter. I then went to the pharmacy to pick up some bandages, adhesive, gauze, and cortisone cream. (I always made sure I had an ample amount of first aid supplies) I was absolutely determined to cause permanent damage to my body that no matter what happened that night, I was not going to divert from the plan to burn myself. My mind set was so strong that I thought this was the only way to deal with the past.

I changed the shirt I was wearing and put on a sleeveless shirt, so I would have plenty of bare skin visible. As I began to drink the first beer, I had a fleeting thought. I remembered that during the last few sessions I promised my therapist and parents that I would call someone when I felt like hurting myself. I already determined that I was going to burn my arm, so I didn't see the point of calling. I knew that no matter what anyone said, nothing would improve. I didn't see my life getting better; I only saw it getting worse.

I finished the beer and quickly drank another before making phone calls. I didn't want to let anyone down, so I called my mother. While I was speaking to her, I drank another beer and lit a cigarette. I took the cigarette and slowly brought it toward my forearm and gently pressed it into my skin. The first cigarette that struck my skin did sting, and then went numb. I pressed it into my forearm until the cigarette went out. I would either re-light the same cigarette or start a new one and continue where I left off. I continued in the same area until I had an indentation, then I would begin a new one. As I continued talking on the phone, I alternated between stabbing cigarettes into my left forearm and slowly pressing them into the skin. After hanging up with my mother, I called my father. I did the same thing while on the phone with him. He didn't ask any questions like my mother, it was just small talk. I eventually got off the phone and went to my room. I glanced at my arm and saw about 13 'holes' in my arm. I didn't obtain the goal that I wanted, so I proceeded to drink some more beer and then got the fire starter. I held my left forearm outward and took the flame close until it went on the skin. As the flame struck my bare skin I flinched and jerked my arm due to the pain. I stopped to figure out how to prevent my arm from moving while I did this. I pushed the dresser close to the window and positioned my arm between the window and the dresser. Once I started again I noticed a dreadful odor in the room and opened the window so that when the owners of the house got home, they were not suspicious.

Just as I got back into position, my cat ran out the window onto the roof. *Oh, this is just great!* I tried to ignore the cat, but somehow got distracted by it. I didn't want her to run away, so I stopped and went through the window onto the roof. She kept running from me. About a half hour later,

I got her back in the room. I kept the window opened, and just placed a towel there so the cat would stay.

Since I was a boarder and no one was home, I was not at all concerned with time. Some of the drunkenness was wearing off, so I drank 5 beers and started again. I made sure the cat was amused and propped up my arm. I continued burning with the lighter until I created a pretty wide mark in my arm.

When I was finished, I put ointment on and bandaged it up. I sat on my bed and fell asleep.

The Morning After

I awoke the next morning to go to my session at the EDU. I went to the shower and as I took off my sweatshirt, I noticed my arm was bandaged. My fingers, hand, and forearm were swollen. *What did you do now?* I took off the bandage and saw about a 5" long by $2\frac{1}{2}$" wide area that was as white as milk and olive green on the outer edges. The area was extremely swollen, though I was not in any pain or discomfort. Even though I was not in any pain, I thought it looked serious. I wasn't quite sure what I should do. I knew if I went to the hospital or emergency room, they may have considered me to be endangering myself and would put me into a psychiatric unit. I got dressed and went to the EDU. When I arrived, I decided to speak with one of the nurses to see what she thought.

I walked over and said, "Uh, hi, uh could you please look at my arm?"

She rolled up my arm and let out a gasp.

I asked her, "What's wrong?"

She turned to me and said, "Vicki, what have you done?"

"I... I...I burned my arm last night."

I remember how sweetly she looked at me that morning.

She turned to me again and asked, "Vicki, did you do this to yourself?"

I looked away and didn't respond.

"It looks pretty serious, you have signs of infection and there is a lot of swelling," she said with concern.

"Alright, can you fix it?" I asked.

"No, Vicki, you don't seem to understand, you need to get that treated right now."

"Oh," I said.

"It looks like a 3rd degree burn to me. You need to go to the emergency room."

"I just want something that will stop the infection," I said.

"You need more than that. This isn't something that is going to heal on its own," she said.

She put some burn cream on my arm, bandaged it and warned me that the doctor would ask how it happened and ask me to have a psychiatric evaluation.

I got my backpack and told her I would be back after visiting the emergency room.

When I arrived at the emergency room, the first thing the nurse asked was how it happened. I figured that all I had to do was stall her, get some ointment or cream to prevent the infection, and leave.

The nurse stared at me and asked again, "How did you do this?"

"I burned it," I said

"How did you burn it?" she asked.

Think quickly. If you tell her that you did it yourself, then you are sure to have a psychiatric evaluation. You better not take the chance of ending up in the hospital.

"Flames were involved," I said.

"Flames, huh?" She didn't seem to have been shocked. I wasn't sure if she was trying to help me or not or if she was just being nice to pacify me. She told me that I had a 3rd degree burn, an infection had begun and that my nerve endings had been damaged. She explained that was why I didn't have any feeling in my arm. She told me that I would require reconstructive surgery.

She handed me burn information and a referral to a surgeon. As she finished cleaning up my arm, she mentioned that I would need to stop by psychiatric services. I walked toward the room, and then left when nobody was paying attention. I was amazed that I left the hospital without a psychiatric evaluation.

On September 21, 1993 I went for an appointment to the plastic surgeon's office. I was placed in a room and examined by Dr. Wolk. When he looked at my arm, he asked if it was a self-inflicted injury. I looked away and didn't answer. He told me he suspected I did it myself. He looked at me and made a humming sound. I'm not quite sure what he was thinking. He never said anything else to me about it, and he didn't contact psychiatric services.

He said that I was in need of reconstructive surgery. He explained that he would remove skin from my upper thigh and attach it to my forearm. A week later I had surgery and was in a cast for several weeks. The cost of the surgery was $1,600.00.

A Mother's Point of View

Shortly after burning my arm, I went to visit my mother and stayed with her for a few days. She took pictures of my arm because she felt that it would keep me from doing it again. While I visited my mother, she was upset because I was not taking care of myself and was sick. It upset her to see me miss doctor visits and check ups. It was so frustrating for her because she didn't want to rub me the wrong way and make me more distant. My judgment was so clouded that I actually thought that I knew the best for myself. My mother was careful with what she said to me because she felt there was no reasoning with me and never knew if she was getting through to me. She said that I was very opinionated. I said that I didn't want any help, but I think deep down I did.

One afternoon, a few years after I burned my arm, my mother told me that I called her many times the night I burned my arm.

"The one time you called me from Clark, New Jersey, you were drunk. You were pretty drunk and I suppose you wanted someone to know you were hurting and deep down you wanted help. I believe it was a huge cry for help. You called me several times that night. I called Dina and asked her to call you, but you never answered the phone that night. During one phone call, I asked if you did anything and you said, 'nothing'. Then in another phone call you told me you were in the midst of burning yourself. I had a visual of you using that fire starter in your little room. These things were so horrifying that I wondered why I didn't call the police. When I hear something that is so beyond reality and so shocking, I just freeze. I remember feeling sick to my stomach and thinking 'what do I do now?' It was beyond my imagination that you could do this to yourself."

Avoid Thoughts That Lead You To Think!

Thinking. Dwelling. Contemplating. That is what I did. It always led me into a path of destruction. I always had flooding thoughts that I felt I couldn't control. I always gave in to what I was thinking. The thoughts always led me to think on other things that would lead me to a place in my head that was out of control.

Every person has the ability to think on just about everything and anything. We can daydream about incredible things. We ponder what it would be like to win a million dollars. We think about the perfect person to marry. Or, we think about the opposite. We think about how miserable we are. We dwell on the past. We consume our thoughts with bad things that happened. We have choices on what to think about. We all have creative minds and can probably think on amazing and wonderful things, however if someone isn't thinking on 'happy thoughts', then they may become engrossed in misery. They may not be able to use their mind and talents as God intended.

We need to get rid of bad thoughts that come into our life. We can do that by not thinking on them or 'fantasizing' about them. Just because a thought enters your mind, doesn't mean that you have to think on it. One of my favorite sayings is 'avoid thinking on things that lead you to think on things that you shouldn't be thinking'. Think about it for a moment. When you are alone, are you content with yourself or do you find yourself thinking about the past abuse, past mistakes, or issues so much that you get fidgety? Is it possible that those thoughts get you full of worry, anxiety, and upset or even depressed?

In that case you may want to avoid thinking on things that lead you to think things that you shouldn't be thinking. This may sound like a tongue twister; however, I believe the saying to be true. Once you think on something negative, it seems that it leads to other negative thoughts and before you know it, you have gotten to a place in your mind that you never intended to get to!

Look at it this way: when you think on something bad, most likely you will begin to feel down and then bad actions follow. However, if you think on good thoughts, those will bring on good actions.

When a bad thought comes (temptations of any kind, past situations, etc.) don't write them down in your mind and keep them with you, instead throw them out.

Avoid thinking on thoughts that lead you to think things that you shouldn't be thinking. This is not the power of positive thinking; this is a biblical principle that God wants for each and every one of us.

When you start to think on good things and read encouraging tidbits like what is contained in the Bible, you will begin to change the way you look at things.

Start thinking on something good. Good thoughts bring on good actions!

CHAPTER 10

THE END IS NEAR

*There used to be times I could think clearly. Now it seems
that I can't think at all. Most of the time I feel like a lifeless
lump. I'm exasperated. I have so much pain inside. I know I
can no longer hide it from anyone. I'm tired of disappoint-
ments. I hate struggling. I hate the voices. I don't want
disorders. Oh, I'm so distraught! I'm tired of living.
Nothing is working! I don't want to go through another
anxiety attack. I don't want to be reliant on medication. I
don't want to go through any of this ever again.
I don't care about anything or anyone anymore. Why
should I? I hate that I can't see beyond my past. I hate that
I don't see a future. I want out of this life.
Journal entry – fall of 1993*

Wanting to Die

A few weeks after having surgery on my arm, I was lying
on my bed thinking about my life. As I looked at the
cast on my arm, I wondered how I ended up where I was. I
couldn't stand the thought of another day. I had been thinking
of killing myself for several weeks and was trying to think of

the best time to do it. I called my brother and told him I hated him and that if I had it in me, I would kill him. I hung up on him and then called Dina and told her I couldn't handle my life anymore. She stayed on the phone with me until I calmed down. She assured me that I would feel better the next day. I told her that if I didn't feel any better, I was going to end it all. I set my alarm for 6:00 a.m. and went to sleep.

When I awoke the next morning nothing changed, in fact, I felt worse. The thoughts seemed as though they were coming from every direction. Since I didn't feel any better, I decided that I would end my life. I had no doubt that I would follow through because I had the same determination I had the day I burned my left arm. Thoughts flooded my mind. I had thoughts that someone was coming after me. *They are coming for you.*

I got dressed, took my backpack, and filled it with all my medication. I had just gotten my prescriptions filled the day before which was a 30-day supply, a little over 500 pills. I knew that if I mixed it all with alcohol, I would surely die. I decided to drive down to Seaside Heights and get a room at the Cetza Hotel. This was the first place that I lived when I first came to New Jersey. This was the only place that was untainted.

Making The Plan Work

As I was driving to the shore, I stopped at a rest stop to call Dina. She asked where I was. I told her that I felt some-one was coming after me. She told me that my therapist and a psychiatric crew showed up at my room at 7:15 a.m., but I had already left. I told her that I couldn't take it anymore or bear to go to another hospital and didn't want to live like this anymore.

"Vic, where are you going?" Dina asked.

"I'm going to the place that I first came to," I answered. I became agitated and slammed down the phone.

On the way down, I stopped off for some beer and rum. When I arrived at the Cetza Hotel, I gave the clerk my credit card and went to a room with a poolside view. I placed my backpack on a chair by the door, grabbed a beer, and put the bag of alcohol on the floor. I went out to get ice to keep the alcohol cold. When I came back, I turned on the television and opened the curtains to the window. I grabbed my back-pack and took all of the medication out of the bottles and carefully placed them on the counter. I separated the pills and categorized them by type. I took the beer and rum over to the sink and placed it on ice. I drank another beer with a handful of medication. I took a swig of rum and then took an additional handful of pills and swallowed them with another beer.

I started on a fourth beer when suddenly, I heard tapping on the window. I glanced over, and there were two uniform police officers at the window. I shut the curtains and asked what they wanted. They said they were called with a report that I might be trying to kill myself. I laughed and said, "If I were trying to kill myself would I do it in front of a big window with the curtains open?" *I guess the answer to this question would be yes, as I was trying to kill myself and the curtains were wide open!*

"Can we come in?" the officer asked.

"Sure," I said. I quickly went to the counter and took as much medication as I could grab and shoved it into my pockets.

I opened the door and the two officers came in and looked around the room.

"How are you doing?" one officer asked.

"I'm doing fine," I answered. They were trying to make small talk, and began poking around. I was trying to keep a cool disposition, but I was getting agitated and angry because they were wrecking my plans.

One of the officers walked over to the sink and asked,

"You have quite a bit of alcohol here, don't you? Isn't it a bit early to drink?"

"No, it's not too early. I'm of legal age and I'm not going anywhere. Why do you care anyway?"

The other officer asked me what the pills on the counter were for. I told him that was my medication for the week and that I was getting it ready.

"Getting ready for what?"

"I take medication. I am just getting it ready. Why are you guys here?"

They proceeded to explain that they received several concerned calls that I was going to kill myself. As they continued to explain, I tuned them out and thought how Dina knew a lot about me. She must have remembered that the Cetza hotel was the first place I lived when I was a little girl! When I realized this, I knew I would have to act quickly if I was going to succeed.

After their explanation, I laughed. "Do I look like I am trying to kill myself?"

The one officer looked around and said, "Well, there is a little bit of evidence that you might be trying to do something here."

"Look, I am having a bad day and am drinking, that's all there is to it."

They told me that when someone places a call regarding a suicide that they are required to follow up. I told them I was fine.

"If you are fine, that's great, will you at least talk with one of the counselors from the suicide hotline?"

"Why don't you talk to one of the counselors instead?" I suggested.

"Because I am not the one who the call is about."

"Look, what's the point?" I asked.

The officer explained to me that they wanted to determine if I was suicidal or not.

I ignored his comments and went over and took a large swig of rum, then opened a beer. Both the officers stared at me.

One officer came toward me. "Don't drink that!"

I smirked at him and said, "Look, I let you in because you are cops. You guys came on in here, and all I'm doing is humoring you, so if you don't like me drinking, well I suppose you could leave."

"Could I look in your backpack?" the officer asked.

"Can I look in yours?" I asked sarcastically.

"I don't have one." he replied.

"Well, then no. No you cannot, you have no reason to look through my things," I said firmly.

I was going nuts in my head and my thoughts were racing. At that point I was just trying to figure a way to get them out of the room. I had yet to finish the pills and needed to get them into my system.

By then a couple other officers had come into the room, and I was getting upset.

As time was passing, all I could think about was taking the remainder of the pills. I couldn't take the pills from the counter because I thought they would get suspicious.

Remembering that I had put some pills in my pocket, I figured I'd go to the bathroom to take them.

"I'll be right back. I'm going to the bathroom."

I grabbed a beer, and the one officer looked at me and asked, "Why are you taking that?"

"To drink," I said as I closed the bathroom door.

I speedily took all the pills out of my pocket and proceeded to swallow them with the bottle of beer.

When I got out of the bathroom, the officers were staring at me.

These guys were really beginning to bother me. I looked at one of the officers and said, "Hey, if you thought I was suicidal, that sure was dumb to let me go to the bathroom.

How do you know I didn't have a gun in there?" Two of the officers scrambled into the bathroom.

A couple of the officers were trying to convince me to talk with psychiatric services. I refused to talk on the phone with their psychiatric services three times, and I guess they realized that I was going to be as persistent as they were.

I was starting to feel a little woozy and tired. I was so close to succeeding, the closest to ending it all as I ever was.

The phone rang and it was Dina's best friend, Todd. "Vicki, look, I know why you are there and what you are trying to do."

"Look Todd you don't know what it's like. I can't live this way anymore."

"I may not have been through what you have, but you can't kill yourself. You have so much to live for."

"Oh really? Okay Todd, I'll play your game. Give me one good reason why I should live, just one."

After a long pause, he said, "Vicki you are so pretty."

"Gee, Todd, is that all you could come up with is 'you're pretty'?"

Todd just gasped and said, "Vic, I've never been in this situation before. All I know is that you are doing everything you can to die and I am doing everything in my power to live." (Todd was dying of AIDS)

He just begged me to talk with the psychiatric services.

When I got off the phone with Todd, I laid on the bed. One of the officers was talking with me and he asked me if I knew if I was going to heaven when I died.

I turned to him and said, "I know you are trying to be nice, but I don't really care about heaven or what you have to say because nothing matters anymore."

"You should care about where you are going."

"Well, the only place I care about going is away from here and not living."

"Jesus loves you."

"Oh, you have got to be kidding me," I said as I looked away.

He grinned and told me that I would be okay.

I was having a tough time focusing. I was slurring my words and I couldn't see well. I spoke with psychiatric services over the phone just as I promised Todd. An ambulance arrived. They told me they were taking me to the hospital for further evaluation. I was placed on a stretcher and was taken to the ambulance. When they lifted me up to the ambulance door, I saw a bright light. In fact, it was the brightest light I had ever seen. My vision was getting clouded and sounds were garbled. The last thing I remember hearing was a woman's voice, "Vicki, can you hear me? Vicki, your fading... your eyes are rolling back. Vicki, did you take something?"

I am not sure exactly how long I was out for, but I woke up around 8:00 p.m. at CMC in Toms River, New Jersey.

A Hopeless Case

When I opened my eyes, I saw my mother at the bedside. I looked up at her, "Oh, Damn!" *Is this nightmare ever going to end!*

"Honey, I love you. Do you know you were minutes away from death? The doctors said you were minutes away, Vic," my mother said as she was crying.

I looked away from my mother. I knew this was hurting her and I didn't want to upset her. There were so many thoughts and emotions going on inside me. I was angry that I was alive. All I thought about was how bad things were and that I had to live through it again. I was a hopeless case. I didn't want to live. I had absolutely no reason to want to be alive. All I could think about was what was behind me. I lived a life of the past. I could not think about the future because that was unknown and scared me too much. I was terrified that the constant torment that I was in would never end.

"Vicki, they gave you charcoal to absorb all the pills. This was close—this was a very close call. Now I know that you really do want to die."

"You're only figuring that out now?" I muttered.

She just put her head down and cried.

One of the counselors had come into the room and was advising me of my options. I had the choice of a private facility, the county's psychiatric unit at KMC, or as a last resort to be committed to the state institution.

The counselor explained that the private facility might not be an option, as my insurance may not cover the costs, due to it being used up from the last hospital stay.

She suggested the county's psychiatric unit.

I turned away and was only partly listening. I was fading in and out due to the medication. She explained to my mother that they could not release me freely, as I was a risk and that I should be willing to at least consider the county's psychiatric unit.

I had no zeal for life and truly didn't care anymore. I didn't care where I went because I wanted to be dead. I dreaded one more session of group therapy.

"I will not go to another hospital!"

"If you don't volunteer to go to the county hospital, you will be committed to the state institution."

"Fine!" I said.

"If you sign yourself to the state institution, your family cannot get you released, you **belong** to the state," she said.

"Like I said, fine. Maybe I'll die there then," I said defiantly.

My mother stepped out of the room with the counselor. My mother came back into the room to talk with me about changing my mind. She talked to me for over an hour begging me to reconsider going to the county's psychiatric unit.

"Honey, you do not want to go be committed. If you go to KMC, you will get good help there, but you will be able to leave after a few weeks. If you go to the state institution you will have no say in your release. I won't even be able to get you out of there," my mother pleaded with me.

"Mom, I don't think you understand. I hate living. I hate my life. I hate who I am. I hate that you love my brother who hurt me for so long. I can't go on living like this. I just can't do it!"

"Please, Vicki, just think about it." She told me that it would work out and that things would change. I am not sure if she really believed that or not, but I am sure she didn't want to see me committed to the state institution and would probably have told me anything to keep me from going there.

I finally gave in and agreed to go to the county's psychiatric hospital. I was admitted to KMC in Lakewood, New Jersey. It was extremely late when I arrived at the hospital. It was dark and dreary and very depressing. I was terrified.

I didn't understand people calling the police that day. I didn't appreciate anything that my mother did that night. I now appreciate all of those who helped me that day and are thankful for all of their efforts. I saw no hope, but they all saw something that I couldn't. I am thankful to God that my mother was there that day talking to the counselors and doctors on my behalf. If she hadn't been there, I would have signed myself to the state hospital.

The police report as follows:

10/5/93 Attempted Suicide - At approximately 1:20 p.m., numerous calls were received by the Seaside Heights police department in reference to an attempted suicide by a female known only as Vicki Freund. It was learned that Ms. Freund was at the Cetza Hotel, possibly in room 204 and that she was operating a pickup truck. Two patrolmen responded to the motel and located the vehicle in the parking lot of the motel. It was confirmed that Ms. Freund was staying in room 204. The two patrolmen along with the motel manager went to room 204. It was observed that there was a white female walking around inside of the room. One of the patrolmen knocked on the door and the female answered. The two patrolmen were allowed into the room. It was observed that there was a large amount of alcohol by the sink in the rear of the room. Ms. Freund stated that she had a large amount of medication on her. After a long conversation with Ms. Freund and with the assistance of the sergeant, Ms. Freund willingly went with the tri-boro first aid squad to CMC to be checked out and later transported for evaluation. A letter was retrieved from Ms. Freund and a copy of that letter was enclosed with the file.

Police Report – Seaside Heights, New Jersey
– October 5, 1993

The Glimmer of Hope!

Have you ever been to a concert or a place where everything goes dark and then everyone turns on a lighter? Instantly, in what was utter darkness is now full of **glimmering light**. Imagine that everyone turns off their lighters, all but one. In that darkness you will be able to see that light flickering, that small glimmer shining through. No matter how dark, that light shines on through and cuts through that darkness, making its light known.

Darkness cannot capture light, no matter how small that light might be.

Sometimes life circumstances can feel as though they are overwhelming, and at times totally unbearable. BUT, just as the light glimmers in the darkest of darkness, **there is hope**. There is hope even in what might appear as the most hopeless of situations.

The next time you have a situation that seems hopeless, or when you think your life offers no hope whatsoever, remember the glimmer of light. Think on how that small glimmer of light breaks through the darkest of darkness.

Then when you see that in your mind, apply that to your situation and realize that even if it is only a glimmer, it is something, and that is hope.

Your light will not burn out; you have hope and a future! Keep holding on to hope, as there is **nothing hopeless**.

> *"For I know the plans I have for you, says the Lord,*
> *thoughts of peace and not of evil, to give you*
> *a future and a hope."*
> *The Bible, Book of Jeremiah, Chapter 29, verse 11*

Whatever you are facing, you can get through it. **Don't give up. God has a plan for you—He really does**.

CHAPTER 11

THE NEVER-ENDING BATTLE

*Here I am, 25 years old living back home with my mother.
I'm on disability and can't work. I know my mother is
trying to help me, but nobody knows how to help me. I am
sick and tired of living my life in fear and torment. I am
finished with therapy. I am done going to group sessions.
I'm tired of rehashing stuff over and over and over and
never getting anywhere! I will not go to another hospital.
They wouldn't understand what I tell them. They would put
me back into the scary places. I don't want to go back. I
won't go back. I can't go back. I think I have become numb.*
Journal entry – fall of 1993

Too Unstable to be Alone

On October 13, 1993 I was released from the KMC in
Lakewood, New Jersey. After being released, I moved
in with my mother. I was not completely thrilled with the
idea of moving in with her after living on my own for 6
years. I also was not happy that I had to rely on someone
else, but it also felt good because I knew that I would be
safe. I didn't trust myself alone. Once I moved in with my

mother, I felt safe with her at the house and I quickly got back into a routine.

Although things actually worsened, I was determined that I would never go back into the hospital again. I made a pact with myself that I would do everything I could to stay out of any type of psychiatric hospital. And, by having that determination, somehow it kept me from wanting to kill myself. My mother refers to my living with her as 'Hell Time'.

There were times I didn't make any progress; it was as if it was to no avail. I was on a self-destructive path. Not only was I harming my body physically, but also I was drinking every night, battling with an eating disorder and was involved in unhealthy relationships. Most of the time I felt numb. I wondered if anyone thought I would ever make it out of this.

My mother was great with me over the next few months; she did everything she could to give me the love and support I needed. She asked me to help her understand why I cut and burn. I couldn't really put it into words, except for telling her that I felt that the pain inside was released when I hurt myself. To explain it better, I showed her some entries in my journal to help her understand. (As outlined in the beginning of chapter 1)

My mother told me that I went through things fast and furious. She felt that I was possessed and told me that there were times she didn't even know who I was. She said there were many times she would talk to me and I would have a glazed look in my eyes, and she had no idea if I comprehended anything.

It got to a point where things were so bad that I thought medication was my answer. I was familiar with all the medication I was taking and knew all the names. If I had a flashback, I took a pill. A bad dream, I took a pill. If I shook too much, I took a pill. If I had an anxiety attack I took a pill.

I had so many instances where I would get upset and cut instantly or have an anxiety attack and cut immediately following. I spent such a long time in therapy without ever getting anywhere. Instead of figuring out what lead to the cutting and what was behind it, I just talked about cutting. There were times that I wasn't really talking about issues that bothered me. There were so many things that would disrupt my life that I would talk about the day-to-day problems without getting to the underlying issues.

Within a week I saw a change in myself and I desperately needed something to control the anxiety, voices, and other things I was dealing with. Being that my mother lived two hours from my therapist, Jan, I began seeing a counselor in the interim.

Things were intensifying, the voices were really strong and I couldn't sleep. Sometimes my mother would come into my bedroom to find me rocking back and forth uncontrollably.

I didn't want to tell my doctor or therapist about feeling the medication was no longer working, because I feared they would have me evaluated, and I would end up in a psychiatric hospital. I decided to self medicate by drinking alcohol. I bought a bottle of rum and hid it in a jacket in my closet. Each evening I would have a glass of rum and pour orange juice with it so that my mother wouldn't notice. It calmed me down; I felt so out of control that I was terrified.

Focusing On A Relationship

Three days after being discharged from KMC, I attended my cousin's wedding and reception. During the reception I met a nice woman, Mara and we exchanged phone numbers. We began to talk almost every night and after about a week we began dating.

Although my mother didn't approve of my lifestyle, she allowed Mara to come over. I knew that deep down she did not accept my relationship with Mara; however, she never commented about it to me. I guess my mother was just content knowing that I was 'happy' in one area of my life.

On Halloween of 1993, Mara invited me to a party at her friend's house. I was struggling the entire day and wasn't comfortable being around people, but I went to make her happy. When we arrived, I saw a razor blade on the kitchen windowsill. When no one was paying attention, I took it and put it in my pocket. Later on in the evening, I went into the bathroom. I took my jacket off and rolled up my shirtsleeve and began to slice up my left arm. I was cutting deeply and accidentally hit a vein, which I sometimes did. The blood began to stream down my arm, onto the sink and the floor. I didn't have any first aid items with me, so I grabbed a roll of toilet paper and put it on my arm. I kept the roll on my arm for a few minutes then wrapped it with half of the toilet paper. I cleaned the razor and the bathroom, and then noticed the bloody roll of toilet paper. I wasn't quite sure how to discard it, so I put it into the garbage can. I took a few pieces of toilet paper and laid them on top of the roll. I rolled my shirtsleeve down and blood was seeping through, I put my jacket on and walked out. I placed the clean razor blade on the windowsill where I found it.

Apparently I didn't clean up as well as I thought, because someone noticed blood in the bathroom. The person went around telling people that there was blood and a roll of bloodied toilet paper in the bathroom. People asked if anyone knew anything about it.

I was afraid to tell Mara because I thought she wouldn't want to be with me anymore.

One evening I showed up at her house later than I was supposed to. I had a black eye and I made up some ridiculous story about pulling over to the side of the road to help someone and how I was hit with a baseball bat. I have no idea if she believed me or not. The truth was that I punched myself in the face earlier that day.

One night I shared with her briefly about my cutting and

she tried to understand, but it overwhelmed her. I showed her my arm where I had burned. She didn't say much about it.

A few weeks later, Mara and her siblings held a surprise party for their parents. I was tending the bar and was sneaking drinks. I drank so much, that mixed with my medication I had a reaction. I started seeing things and hearing voices strongly. I flipped out. I ran out into the hallway and started yelling. I was not sure where I was. I ran outside and started tearing at my shirt, threw it to the ground, and tossed around my shoes. I ran across a field, over a highway, and ran into a building where I found a payphone. I was at a police station.

I remember being at the payphone dialing and Mara grabbed me and took me out of the police station. I sent her flowers to apologize, but she was very upset with me. I mean what could I say, "Hey Mara, I have mental illness, and some days are good and others I don't even remember my own name." I'm sure that she would not have responded well to that. I really cared for her, and I wanted to get close to her, but I was too afraid that it would freak her out and that she would not want to be around me.

Based on previous experiences, I became accustomed to people being in my life for a couple months and then leaving. It seemed as soon as I got close to someone, for some reason they would vanish out of my life. It became easier to put up a wall, a little lonelier, but easier.

Rather than face confrontation, I would run and hide from it. It was easier to do than to hear what someone had to say. I was afraid to hear the truth and or someone's opinion.

Are You a Runner?

You know that statement, "When the going gets tough, the tough get going?"

Are you the type of person who stays around when things get rough or are you the type of person that runs when things get tough?

When difficulties come our way, it is easier to run away and leave the situation than it is to stay around and wait for it to be resolved.

It takes a strong person to face the tough circumstances in life, a responsible person to face the situation that they are in, and a patient person to stay in challenging circumstances and see the end result through.

These are all great qualities to possess:
- **Strength**
- **Patience**
- **Responsibility**

Take a walk through the crisis rather than running away from it.

It may not be easy to face conflicts or difficulties. In fact, the challenge is to **stay around to face the troubles of life,** as running is the easy way out. To stay around and 'face the music' seems to be the hard way, but you will have so much more success than if you ran from it.

Whether you put yourself in a difficult situation or are there due to the actions of another, you will eventually gain strength and peace by facing the problem and getting through it.

Take off those running shoes and put on those walking shoes!

CHAPTER 12

TRYING TO COPE

Change! Another change! Oh, how I hate changes. This is
the day I moved! Mom and Dina helped me move in. I
couldn't take it. I sat in my truck hitting my head against
the steering wheel. I tried to keep it together in front of
them, but I didn't. I don't know what prompted me. My
mom was outside the truck and I just started beating my
head. I think mom asked me to stop. I stopped when Dina
came to talk to me then started when she walked away.
This was another disruptive time in my life. Everything that
is happening is a disappointment and upheaval. I'm afraid
to get close to anyone. Eventually the 'real me' is going to
come out. I want friends. I want to be liked. I don't want
to be who I am. I want to be normal. I want the
flashbacks to cease. I just want to live a normal life.
Would I recognize normal? I have no clue.
Journal entry – winter of 1994

Moving Away

I accumulated a lot of debt due to various doctor and
hospital bills and claimed bankruptcy in January of

1994. Toward the end of January, Mara stopped calling and she eventually broke up with me. I don't actually remember the breakup occurring.

I moved out from my mother's house in February of 1994. My mother and Dina helped me move into a one-bedroom apartment. I went back to work at the athletic store where I was demoted to an assistant manager.

I always feared that someone was in my apartment. Every time I would come home, I would turn on all of the lights and check all the closets, the bathroom, behind the shower curtain, and under the bed. After I would check these places, I would recheck them. I felt that if the lights were on I would be safe.

The anxiety attacks were awful; sometimes I couldn't remember where I was or what I was doing. I would rehearse over and over again in my head what had occurred. The more I would think on things, the worst things became.

I would go shopping for knives, bandages, thread for stitches, and other supplies. Once I would harm myself, I would get disgusted at what I did and throw everything in the garbage. I would keep repeating the process, over and over; go out and buy knives and first aid supplies and then throw them away after using them.

I always kept a knife, razor, or blade in a variety of secret hiding places just in case I had gotten the urge to cut.

My emotions, thoughts, and choices varied from day to day. One day could be relatively okay, and the next could be devastating. The cutting intensified and I found myself drinking more beer and rum than ever.

Let the Hammer Fall

One day while at work, I had the thought of breaking the bones in my left hand by smashing it with a hammer. The more I tried to fight the thoughts, the stronger the feelings got. I dwelled on it for a week when I planned to do it. I bought enough alcohol to numb myself, and bought a new hammer. I knew it would take more alcohol than when I burned my arm because these were bones and were different than that of nerve damage.

As I got all of my supplies, there was something tugging at me not to do it. *How will you explain this at the hospital? How can you say breaking your bones is an accident?* I feared going back to the hospital. I remembered the pact I made with myself that I would never go into another psychiatric unit again. Then, it was as if something was pulling at me to do it. *You have to do this! You already bought the stuff. You said you were going to do it. You can't turn back now. You don't want to look like a failure!* I kept going over and over again in my mind what I would say when asked how my bones got broken, seeing marks of a hammer imprinted on my skin.

I had the hammer in my hand and as I brought it up and toward my hand, I stopped quickly before it reached my skin. At that moment I changed my mind. I had mixed emotions about the whole thing. There was part of me that felt victorious that I had overcome those feelings, but another part of me felt guilty that I didn't hurt myself; almost like a failure. To make up for he damage I saved by not breaking the bones in my hand, I felt that I had to hurt myself in some way. I grabbed a butcher knife and cut my bicep.

It seemed as though things would be okay for a day or two but then would change. No matter what I tried to do, I always reverted back to the same old thing.

Burned Again

On March 22, 1994, I was sitting in my living room and was just thinking. It didn't take much to get me thinking about anything, but this time I was thinking about the destruction I had done to my body. I noticed four small pieces of graphite (pencil lead) in my arm and then thought of all that I had done to myself. *In less than a year you have taken a nail clipper to gouge skin out of your wrist, removed a tooth, hit and punched yourself to no avail, stabbed with anything available, cut with the sharpest knives and razor blades you could get your hand on, and burned your own flesh in an indescribable way. What is all of this doing? Where are you going in life? There has got to be more to life than just existing. There has to be. There just has to be.* As I sat back, I became very somber and looked at my arms and legs and then noticed that my right arm was scar free.

At that moment I decided to burn my right arm. I wanted to mark up that part of me since it had never been touched before. I went out and bought beer, rum, cigarettes, and a lighter. When I got back I grabbed the phone and the phone number to the psychiatric hotline. This time was different than the first time I burned my arm in that I wanted to be stopped this time. There was something inside of me that didn't want to go through with it.

I phoned the counselor and she was unhelpful and unfriendly. I told her she should definitely never go into the line of work of customer service. I felt more like I was on a telemarketing call than someone in need of help. When I got off the phone I felt like hurting myself more than when I started. All the thoughts of not wanting to do it and wanting to be stopped came to a quick halt. I quickly drank a few beers and some rum and gathered all my supplies. I sat on the couch in the living room and began to attack my arm with cigarettes just as I had done six months earlier. Once I had 9 'holes' I burned it with a barbeque lighter. When I was finished I went into the bathroom and bandaged my arm. When I came back to the living room, I was angry and I threw the cigarettes and lighters all over the room.

The next day, I awoke to swollen fingers, hand, and forearm. There was a 4" long by 2" wide area that was as white as milk and olive green on the outer edges. The area was extremely swollen, though I was not in any pain or discomfort. This was very similar to when I burned my left arm. I knew if I went to the hospital or emergency room, they may have considered me to be endangering myself and would put me into a psychiatric unit. I knew I wasn't suicidal so I went to the emergency room to have my arm looked at.

A nurse looked at my arm and told me that I had a 3rd degree burn, an infection had begun, and that my nerve endings had been damaged. She told me that it would require reconstructive surgery. She handed me burn information and a referral to a surgeon. As she finished cleaning up my arm, the nurse walked me to psychiatric services for an evaluation.

I was there for several hours but later released. It was recommended that I keep my appointment with my therapist, Jan and it was also suggested that I increase my sessions with her. I was prescribed to take my medication and given instructions for my burn. I was told that if at any time I become suicidal or felt like the need to self mutilate, I should call the hotline or return to Psychiatric Emergency Services. I was not suicidal but calling that hotline made me feel that way. *No, I'll call the hotline if I want to feel suicidal.* Going for a psychiatric evaluation felt routine. It was as if I could playback exactly what the doctors or nurses would say to me.

A few days later I went for an appointment to the plastic surgeon's office. When Dr. Wolk walked into the room and examined my arm he asked if this was a self-inflicted injury. As I had done before, I looked away and didn't answer. He told me that he hoped I would get help and that he didn't want to see me again. Like he had done before, he didn't say anything more to me about it, and he didn't contact psychiatric services.

He told me that I was in need of reconstructive surgery and that he would remove skin from my upper right thigh and attach it to my forearm. A week later I had surgery, and was in a cast for several weeks. The surgery cost another $1,600.00.

I made up some ridiculous story to my place of work which I am not sure if they believed or not. After the cast came off, I covered my arms with white ace bandages and hoped nobody would notice that I was out of control again.

One Night Stand

There were times that one bad choice followed another. On an evening in April of 1994, rather than drink alone, I went to a local bar where I knew the bartender. After closing, the bartender, Paul was invited to his friend Elena's house with a small group of people and asked me to come along. Elena introduced herself and asked me to drive with her. As we walked to her car, I noticed that she was incredibly beautiful and very muscular. When we arrived at her apartment, Elena showed me some pictures and ribbons on the wall of horses that she rode. She told me that she was an equestrian and would be moving back to Russia to her fiancé. After we talked for a little while, I went back to the living room and the only one awake was Paul, the others were lounged over the couches. We chatted for a few minutes when I heard a whisper of my name. As I turned around, I saw Elena waving me over to her.

I got up and walked over to her. She took me by the hand and walked me down the hall, out of sight to the others. She placed her hand on my face and kissed me. I was totally surprised. She took me into her bedroom and shut and locked the door.

Around 5:00 a.m. I got up, and as I was getting dressed she asked where I was going. I told her that I needed to go home. She walked me to the door, gave me her phone number and kissed me goodbye.

The next day I called her but there was no answer. A few

more days passed and as I was walking past the post office, I noticed Elena's' black car parked in the front of the post office. I walked in and I saw her at the counter. When I approached her she was addressing a letter and barely looked up at me.

She told me she had to go and walked out. This just added to my list of insecurities and low self-esteem. The realization that I was just used didn't occur to me. I am not sure why I slept with her or anyone else for that matter. I guess in some way I thought by sleeping with someone, they would like me and want to be around me.

When I got home, I boiled water and poured it on my left hand several times. I kept it bandaged for several days and never went to the hospital.

Relationships are choices

It is interesting how relationships, good and bad, can influence your thoughts, views and decisions. One doctor at a psychiatric hospital told me that he thought almost all the relationships I was in were unstable. He also said that I should be careful of the romantic relationships I get involved in during my recovery. He believed that I would focus on the other person, and put all my energies toward him/her rather than my problems or issues. I found that to be true, as when the relationship ended, I was traumatized and it set me off into a path of destruction.

There were many dysfunctional relationships that I got into rather than focus on my problems. I looked to others for attention and satisfaction. It was a false sense of security. Interestingly enough, there were countless times in my life that it seemed that I intentionally put myself in potentially dangerous situations. I said yes to things that I should have said no to. It seemed that at times I lost all understanding of good judgment and my perception was impaired. If that is the case with you, then find someone good in your life who can make a good decision and ask them if what you are about to do is good or bad.

When we say YES to the wrong things and to everything that comes our way, that can be an opening to a potential problem. Be careful when saying YES to everything. You don't want to become so consumed with pleasing people that you lose all sense of who you are and become what others want you to be. Remember, if you cannot make a decision, then find someone in your life who can make a good decision and ask them if what you are about to do is good or bad.

When You Don't Remember

One evening in May of 1994, I phoned Dina telling her I was very upset and she came over. By the time she arrived, I had taken a knife and slashed my neck several times. The only thing I vaguely remember is opening the door seeing Dina shocked.

Although I don't remember all that took place that evening, when I awoke the next morning, I saw my bloodied clothes on the floor, my bloody handprints along the wall, blood in the bathroom sink and on the mirror. Dina called me that morning and told me when I opened the door my clothes were full of blood and I had a bloody knife in my hand. She said she helped me change my clothes and put me to bed.

Unfortunately, this was not the first time this occurred. There were many times that I woke up to blood as a result of a self-inflicted wound from the night before.

This particular incident terrified me, as I was terrified that I would accidentally cut a vein and die. I contacted Jan, my therapist and she convinced me that it would be a good idea to go to the hospital to think things through and calm down. I went to the hospital that morning prior to going to work. While I was being evaluated, they asked me why I cut my neck. I told the counselor that I did not recall cutting my neck.

"Did you contact the helpline?"

"No, I didn't."

"Why not?"

"Because I didn't think I was in any danger."

"Do you still feel like killing yourself?"

"I don't want to kill myself. I am not suicidal."

I came to find out that I missed my jugular vein by a few millimeters.

I tried to cover up the cuts on my neck, but I couldn't. I went to work and within a few days was fired. I asked why and was told, 'You know why'. I did not know why, but left anyway.

Losing my job intensified my feelings toward doing harm to my body. I was unemployed and soon on food stamps and had government assistance for a short time. I began to use credit cards as a means of getting by and not before too long; I accumulated quite a bit of debt. My therapist thought it would be a good idea to have more sessions and also add a weekly group session since I was now free during the week.

My mother remembers so much from that time. "There were some horrifying times when you would call me and be totally distraught and depressed. You would give hints that you were going to hurt yourself. You didn't always tell me, but that one time you burned your left arm you told me while you were doing it. Most of what you did was too much for me to comprehend."

Things Turning Around

It was highly recommended that I start working again as Jan felt that I had too much idle time. I took her suggestion, and in September of 1994 I started a temporary position at a book warehouse. I was struggling, but seemed to do better while I was working.

I knew someone who knew of a prestigious company in the area that was hiring for the holiday season. In November I went on the interview and miraculously got the job. I started working there and was doing fairly well.

On February 1, 1995, I realized I couldn't handle living alone and moved in to a 3-bedroom apartment with my friend, Ray and his friend Mark.

When I was 26 years old, in the middle of March of 1995, I went to church for the first time in over 10 years. In June I bought a two-month-old pit bull puppy and named him Micah. Over the next few months I was becoming responsible, gained clarity, focus, insight and a zeal for life. I began to see that there was hope!

The Necklace in the Well!

Has your issue been buried by other problems and unhealthy coping mechanisms? Are you at a point where you just want to be numb? Whether you said yes to all or one, let me tell you about the necklace in the well.

Imagine you have a beautiful necklace in your hand and you go over to a well. As you are bending to look inside, the **necklace accidentally drops** into the well and it falls to the bottom. You want to go in after it, but you are **not sure how to get it out**. You ponder for a moment and realize in order to get the necklace out of the well you would get wet and you might get hurt, so you decide to let it stay at the bottom of the well.

Every now and then you go and look inside the well and you see the necklace has started to change in appearance. Over the years you notice that you can **barely see your necklace**, as there have been other things that were thrown into the well. A few more years pass and you can no longer see your necklace, as there is a cloud in the water from the muck and mire and other debris that made their way into the well. You then think to yourself, "If I had only gotten my necklace when it fell, I would have it."

Your problem is like the necklace in the well. Whatever the traumatic issue was, it has become buried by other things; **buried by other problems** as a result of the 'real issue' like unhealthy coping mechanisms such as cutting, drinking, drugs, anorexic or bulimic behavior.

The **issue will not go away by avoiding it**. By letting your problem just lay dormant, it is only going to get covered up and cluttered by other things. As time goes by you may not even know what the real issue is because so many other problems have risen as a result of never dealing with the issue from the beginning.

Thinking about the work that would go into facing your issue and getting it out of your mind and heart may seem more overwhelming than just to leave it buried there.

Had the necklace been taken out of the well as soon as it was dropped, you could have done with it what you wanted, rather than having it get all tainted. Thinking about the work that would go into getting the necklace may have seemed more tedious than it was worth, as you may not have thought how it would affect you in the long run.

Just like the necklace, being left there at the bottom covers up the issue. Now, in order to get to the necklace you have to go through all the other junk to get to it. Thankfully, that is where you take it at your own pace, one little accomplishment at a time.

You are worth something, and no matter how long your necklace has been at the bottom of the well, it is never too late to get it out!

All things are possible to those that believe. You just have to believe and take action!

CHAPTER 13

OLD THINGS BECOME NEW

This is amazing! Is this what life is all about? This is terrific. I can enjoy things. I am actually happy. I can think clearly. Ever since I stopped my medication a few months ago, I have never felt better. I feel like a new person. When I get sad, I know it is not the end of the world—it is just for the moment and will pass. Wow! All these years, I wrote in a journal, just writing to cope, to escape, in some way to make sense of my life. Today, I write to you, God, giving you thanks for saving me and healing me!
Journal entry – March of 1996

The Start of Something New

Although I occasionally went to Sunday mass as a little girl, I really didn't have a religious or church-going background. I didn't have any godly teaching, so when I became a Christian in 1995 I really just took the Bible at face value. When I started reading that Jesus heals, **I believed it and expected Him to do it.** In June of 1995 I began attending church on a regular basis. It was a church that taught the Bible clearly, believed in healing; that God still heals today, and that He is real.

One day in July of 1995, I decided to stop going to therapy. A few days later I took all of my medication and flushed it down the toilet. I am not suggesting anyone to do that—this is what I did and what I felt led to do at the time. After I stopped going to therapy and stopped taking medication, I asked God to take anything that was not of Him out of me and to give me desires for Him and for good things. Over a period of time, the negative desires went away.

How and When I Changed

In April of 1996, when I was 27 years old, I thought it would be a good idea to spend time alone to pray. At that time, my church had a room available for prayer from 6:00 a.m. to 3:00 p.m. I used to get up at 5:00 am almost every morning to go to the gym before going to work. I started to go to prayer during that time instead of going to the gym. I'm not exactly sure what prompted me, but I thought it would be a good idea. For the next 2 years, I went there four times a week for two hours and just talked to God, prayed, sang, and read my Bible. It was like I was getting to know God and He was 'fixing' me. That time alone changed my life. Whatever problems and issues I had, they were leaving. All the negative desires left. I no longer harm myself in any way. I don't struggle with an eating disorder. I no longer have mental disorders. I have forgiven each person who harmed me. I have peace with my life and I no longer live in fear or in the past, I have joy.

Cleaning out the Closet

In February of 1997, when I was 28 years old, I was ready to live on my own and moved out to a garage apartment. It was a small place, the size of a one-car garage, but I was happy to be on my own. In my eyes it was a castle. I was so content. I was full of joy being able to be alone and wasn't scared. I was so peaceful and enjoyed the solitude for the first time that I could remember!

When I was unpacking, I noticed my 'secret box'. It was a box that contained items from past relationships. Throughout the years I kept all sorts of items from relationships. I kept all the pictures of anyone who I dated along with greeting cards, letters, and jewelry. I also kept an itemized list of any person I had a relationship or any type of sexual encounter with. I'm not sure why I made a list, but I kept the list for years. I kept it all in a box and took it with me every time I moved. I opened the box and looked at what I had inside. There were so many memories: good, bad and indifferent. I held on to so much and wondered why I kept all those things for so long.

I realized that in order for me to continue going forward, I needed to truly let go of all my past relationships. I wanted a fresh start, so I decided that I didn't need all of those things from my past. It was a life I no longer lived. I took all the letters and greeting cards outside, placed them on the driveway and burned them. I tore up all the pictures and threw them away. I took all the clothes that were in good condition and gave them away; leather jackets, boots, suits, jewelry and skates. I got rid of everything that was ever given to me from a relationship.

Starting To Succeed

Within the next few years at the company I worked for, I started to succeed. I received pay increases and did exceedingly well. In the spring of 1998, I was promoted to a position that required a Master's degree, which I didn't have any education past high school. I began working in the Human Resource department as a trainer and within a few months, trained hundreds of employees. I designed and developed training programs that I never thought possible.

The Husband of My Prayers

In the summer of 1998, I began to talk with a man, Chris from my church who I had acquaintance with for 3 years. Within a few weeks, on September 8, 1998 Chris asked me if I would like to go out one afternoon for lunch. When we began talking, I was amazed at his kindness and how peaceful he was.

When we went out for a second time, he took me to a nice restaurant. We were discussing our relationship and where it was going. As we were eating, he told me, "The next woman I kiss is going to be my wife. And it will be when we get married that we kiss, not while we are seeing one another."

I gasped and nearly choked on my food. Then he continued by telling me there would be no physical contact while we were seeing one another. This was so new to me. *A man who didn't want to touch me? What was wrong with him?* It is odd that I thought something was wrong with him, when in actuality everything was right with him.

A few weeks later, Chris asked if he could hold my hand. Of course I said yes. He said, "The holding of hands represents the interlocking of love between us. I love you. And, I look forward to loving you more."

A few weeks later, on October 23, 1998 when I was 30 years old, we had been seeing one another for six weeks when he told me he wanted to take me away for the weekend. He took me to Newport, Rhode Island to see the beautiful mansions. We had separate rooms at a bed and breakfast. When we were going to our rooms to go to sleep, Chris mentioned that he would like to get up to see the sunrise. The next morning at 6:00 a.m. Chris knocked on my door and I was tired and told him I was going back to sleep. At 8:00 a.m. he came back knocking and I got up and we had breakfast. We went for a walk along the harbor and as soon as we got there, he asked if we could sit down because he wanted to tell me something. As I sat down, he got down on one knee and professed his love to me and asked me to marry him. I said yes!

After we were engaged, I told him that I wanted to share some things with him. I talked with him in detail about the happenings in my life. I shared with him about my abusive past, my battles with mental disorders, and causing harm on my body. He said, "That may have been who you were, but that is not who I see now." I was apprehensive about him seeing me without clothes or in a bathing suit because my scars would be revealed. He told me that no matter how obvious they might seem, he will not notice them because he doesn't see the scars when he looks at me.

We were married 6 months later on April 24, 1999. To this day, Chris tells me that he does not see any marks on my body when he looks at me. That is love!

Chris makes me incredibly happy, is a wonderful husband, and I am so thankful for him. We bought a house and are looking forward to starting a family. It is so marvelous at how God has turned my life around.

A Way of Helping Others

I finally was at the point that I could help others. In August 2001, I created a self-help website entitled, End ALL The Pain! (www.endallthepain.com) It was created to make available much needed information on an assortment of issues and to provide support for those who have experienced painful and traumatic situations in one way or another. Another objective is to provide an encouraging, understanding, and healthy place to go for the tough questions you have regarding what you have experienced, or what you may be going through right now.

In January of 2003 I was asked to visit a teenage girl, J in a psychiatric unit who intentionally cut herself. It was there that I met and spoke with other teens that harmed themselves.

Over the next few months, I began spending time with two of the girls, LB and D, whom I grew to adore. I discussed godly things, which in itself was a challenge; visited them, spent many late nights talking, and even bandaged up their self-inflicted wounds. I believe the time we share will have a lasting effect. I continue to make myself available to anyone who harms, as the opportunity presents itself.

Replacing Old with New

I needed to change old habits. I slowly learned that once something negative is taken away, it needed to be replaced with something positive. For example, replace alcohol and drugs with a good recovery program, replace hanging out at the wrong places with alternative activities, replace friends that brought you down with healthy relationships, and replace your idle time with activities that keep the mind occupied.

This would be extremely simple if our will wasn't involved. I mean, seriously, think about it, were you ever around a kid who gets curious and wants to get into something he shouldn't, like touch a hot pot or a hot burner? The parent tells him NO, and he asks why. The parent explains that he will get hurt if he touches it. Then, he gets all the more curious and touches it when the parent is not looking and screams because he just burned his fingers! We (people) are like that. We get to a point where we know what to do, but choose to do something else. It's our choice, because we don't 'feel' like doing what we should.

For example, instead of praying, we watch a movie, instead of going to church we sleep in, instead of being around good influences, we go hang out with people who bring us down, instead of listening to uplifting music we listen to depressing songs that ultimately bring us down. Then we wonder why we aren't getting answers, why we don't have this or why we don't have that, or we feel that God has left us, or that this 'faith thing' doesn't work, etc.

That Was Then and This is Now!

Years ago I thought I had a good reason to beat myself up, pull my hair out and cut and burn my body. I was greatly deceived. I now have a good reason to show my scars and to tell other people about it. I hope that everyone who reads my story will know that they can get through anything! If you are struggling with anything that I have discussed, know you can get through it just like I did and lead a normal, healthy life **as God intended for you!**

I kept what people did to me a secret. I wouldn't tell anyone because I was told not to tell and I became scared. When I was sexually abused as a child, I waited 6 months to tell my mother. When my brother abused me, I waited 6 years from when it first began. When my uncle raped me, I waited almost 4 years until I said anything. No matter what you go through, tell someone. If a person harms you or abuses you, go and tell someone. **Go and tell** because someone cares for you!

Did someone ever call you on the telephone, but you were not at home to answer the call or you just didn't feel like answering? Well, that doesn't mean the person didn't call you, it just meant that you either weren't around to take the call or you made a choice not to answer. It is the same thing with God: He was always calling me, but I didn't answer. I always wondered why God wasn't there for me, but He was there the whole time. I know that God loves me. He loved me years ago and He loved me while I was going through my problems. And, He loves you!

As you read this book, I hope you are encouraged to overcome whatever you have going on in your life, as **nothing is hopeless!** I firmly believe that people have the ability to overcome every hardship and conquer what they may be going through. It may take some work, but you can do it.

At times facing recovery may seem challenging, but most definitely worth every effort. It may seem difficult periodically, but know that you are not alone. Don't give up, not for a second and keep fighting to win the race!

For those who are doing anything negative, think about reigning in your mind, will, and emotions. Try and throw the negative thoughts out of your mind, submit your will to the will of God and prevent being led by your emotions. It might sound easier said than done, but it is possible! You might even want to go out and get a Bible and start reading it. You never know what can happen when you start reading! Take a moment and think about opening your heart to God. Ask God to change you. Ask God to help you. He will touch you—He will heal you—He will change you—He is just a prayer away!

But what does it say? "The word is near you, in your mouth and in your heart" (that is, the word of faith which we preach) that if you confess with your mouth the Lord Jesus and believe in your heart that God has raised Him from the dead, you will be saved. For with the heart one believes unto righteousness, and with the mouth confession is made unto salvation.

The Bible, Book of Romans, Chapter10, verses 8-10

Whatever you have gone through or may be facing right now, you can get through it as I did and **lead a normal healthy life as God intended for YOU!**

Contact Information:
End All The Pain!
Vicki F. Duffy
P.O. Box 194
Florham Park, NJ 07932 U.S.
www.endallthepain.com

Printed in the United States
97072LV00001B/122/A

9 781594 675423